LINGUISTICS AND PSEUDO-LINGUISTICS

AMSTERDAM STUDIES IN THE THEORY AND

HISTORY OF LINGUISTIC SCIENCE

General Editor
E.F. KONRAD KOERNER
(University of Ottawa)

Series IV - CURRENT ISSUES IN LINGUISTIC THEORY

Volume 55

Robert A. Hall, Jr.

Linguistics and Pseudo-Linguistics

LINGUISTICS AND
PSEUDO-LINGUISTICS
SELECTED ESSAYS
1965-1985

ROBERT A. HALL, Jr.
Cornell University

JOHN BENJAMINS PUBLISHING COMPANY
AMSTERDAM/PHILADELPHIA

1987

Library of Congress Cataloging in Publication Data

Hall, Robert Anderson, 1911-
  Linguistics and pseudo-linguistics.

(Amsterdam studies in the theory and history of linguistic science. Series IV, Current issues in linguistic theory, ISSN 0304-0763; v. 55)
Bibliography: p.
Includes index.
1. Generative grammar. 2. Deconstruction. I. Title. II. Series.
P158.H28   1987   415   87-21053
ISBN 90 272 3549 X (alk. paper)

In Memoriam

W. FREEMAN TWADDELL

(1906-1982)

CONTENTS

Robert Anderson Hall, Jr.

PREFACE AND ACKNOWLEDGEMENTS

Although the intellectual impulse behind the transformational-generative grammar (TGG) movement of the 1960's and 1970's is by now largely spent, the use of TGG as a weapon in academic power-politics is unfortunately still wide-spread. The same is true of the (not unrelated) "deconstructionist" movement in literary criticism. It is, therefore, still appropriate to present, as energetically as possible, the case against TGG and "deconstructionism," to expose the harm they have done to linguistics and to literary criticism, respectively.

With this aim in mind, I have therefore gathered in this volume twelve of my essays, published between 1965 and 1985. The first ten contain animadversions on various aspects of TGG; the last two, on Derridian deconstructionism, especially insofar as it is based on an erroneous and untenable conception of language. I hope that the considerations presented in these articles and book-reviews will persuade the reader to look on both of these approaches with a critical eye.

I have left the essays pretty much as they were written, with only a few additions (mostly to mention significant later developments) and a few rectifications of errors. In one or two instances, there are minor typographical discrepancies between articles (e.g. in the use of single or double quotation-marks). There are some repetitions from one article to the next (e.g., in my definitions of theology, science, and religion), which I have not excised, since most users will probably be referring to the essays separately, rather than treating them as a continuous span for reading at a single sitting. All the references, however, have been gathered together in one listing at the end of the volume.

For permission to reprint these articles and reviews, I am indebted to the editors and publishers of the various journals as indicated under each title.

Ithaca, N.Y.   R.A.H. jr.
April 1987

FACT AND FICTION IN GRAMMATICAL ANALYSIS

(Foundations of Language 1.337-345 [1965])

The term FICTION, in the title of this paper, does not have any pejorative sense. FICTIONS are referred to here in the same sense as they are by Hans Vaihinger in his *The Philosophy of 'As If'*: 'hypotheses which are known to be false, but which are employed because of their utility'.[1] A fiction of this kind can be used successfully (and hence legitimately) in scientific investigation if it is either removed before the end of the process or cancelled out by an opposing fiction (what Vaihinger calls 'the method of antithetic error'.[2] If, on the other hand, a fiction is allowed to affect the final formulation of the results of analysis, without being removed or cancelled out, its continued presence will falsify our findings. It is my purpose in this paper to examine briefly certain fictions which enter into the current practice of transformational and other types of grammar,[3] and the extent to which their use is helpful or harmful to language-analysis and -learning.

I. SOME FICTIONS

A. SYNCHRONICITY. Work on the synchronic axis of language-description necessarily involves a fiction which is patently quite unrealistic, but very helpful, namely that it is possible to eliminate from our investigation all irreversible changes in linguistic structure, and to describe this latter as if no time were passing. There are two types of time involved: that which passes while the language is being used by its speakers, and that which passes while the observer is passing from one feature to another in his observation and description of the language. All synchronic approaches share the fiction that the first kind of time-factor can be eliminated. That the second kind is at all times to be eliminated, is the fiction which underlies the 'item-and-arrangement' (IA) model of language-description.[4] The end-product of this type of description is in some ways comparable to a geographical map, which likewise presents its subject-matter as if it were wholly unchanging and could be taken in at a single glance.[5] When applied rigorously, the IA approach produces a completely static description: even the most obvious 'grammatical processes' are stated in terms of a timeless relationship, often requiring much more complicated and tortuous formulation than would the simple statement of a 'process.'[6]

The 'item-and-process' model (IP) shares with the IA approach the basic fiction of synchronicity in the subject-matter, linguistic structure, but it involves a different fiction concerning the passage of time for the observer: that this passage of time MUST be taken into account, and hence that the difference between one i-tem and another is to be described as if a change had taken place from one to the other (as if the observer could never take in more than one item at a time). In the statement of any given 'process', this fiction covers only the relation between the particular items involved; and most descriptive grammars that are not of the rigor-ously IA type make more or less extensive, but still relatively un-systematic, use of grammatical 'processes' in their formulations.[7] Transformational grammar extends the fiction of a necessary passage of time for the observer to the entire description, and makes it basic to its presentation. (Transformational grammar is, in a way, the revenge taken by IP over IA for the latter's extensive predomi-nance.) The result of a thorough-going transformational description is comparable to a guide-book rather than to a map; the aim of such a guide is to give instructions for proceeding through the entire area in such a way as to pass quickly, conveniently, and economi-cally from one point to the next.

      B. UNIDIRECTIONALITY. Both 'phonological grammars' (those starting with phonology and working 'upwards' to morphology and syntax) and transformational and other grammars which start at the 'top' with syntax, and work 'downwards', share the fiction that de-scription is to proceed, if not exclusively, at least primarily in one direction. 'Feed-back' is normally permitted from stages al-ready passed, but not anticipation of levels or material not yet touched.   In actual human behavior, all 'levels' of linguistic structure exist at the same time and unquestionably interact with each other in all directions. Any decision on the analyst's part to ignore such co-existence and interaction rests on the (admitted-ly useful) fiction that they can be ignored.

      C. BINARY CHOICE. That every step in a process of description must be framed in terms of an 'either-or' alternative is a fiction which is quite useful for certain types of work, especially with machines which operate on this very principle.[8] There are certain subsidiary fictions that grow out of this one: e.g. that transfor-mations must proceed by single steps, including (if necessary) in-termediate steps which do not correspond to any reality in the lan-guage, but are 'logical' necessities for getting from one construc-tion to another, or even starting with non-existent constructions, as in the sequence:[9]

         *The motor is for for the motor to drive the shaft. →

         *The motor is for for to drive the shaft. →

         *The motor is for to drive the shaft. →

         The motor is to drive the shaft.

A further fiction, arising out of that of obligatory binary choice, has aroused considerable discussion because of its rather obviously fictitious nature: that of 'ungrammaticality', the assumption that

the end-out-put of a transformational process must be either wholly
acceptable or wholly unacceptable. As a result of fairly strong
criticism on this point,[10] the original, completely 'either-or'
formulation of this principle has been modified to admit (in theory) a range of 'semi-grammatical' constructions which might be produced by a native speaker;[11] yet the notion of completely 'ungrammatical or totally inadmissible results still remains.

D. WRITING 'VERSUS' SPEECH. Although transformationalists
have given lip-service to the existence of sound as a necessary
part of language, and have even published discussions of the rôle
of phonology (including intonation) in a transformational grammar,[12] their practice has nevertheless been based very largely on
the fiction that language is to be formulated primarily in terms of
writing rather than speech. This assumption is seen even in the
almost universal description of transformations as involving 're-
writing', and of the necessary rules as being 're-write'-rules.
At best, these expressions are merely somewhat unfortunate equiva-
lents for 'reformulation' and 'principles of reformulation' respectively; at worst, they imply that sound is an unessential part of
language, as compared to writing. Yet phonation is an integral
part of the linguistic behavior of normal humans, as are listening
to speech and interpreting it (as has been shown by studies on sub-
vocalization).[13]

II. USEFULNESS OF FICTIONS

Each of the above-mentioned fictions is admittedly useful, in
some instances essential, in certain respects. The modification of
synchronicity to require a fictionally necessary passage of the observer from one item to the next enables many awkward and over-com-
plicated formulations of the IA type to be avoided. Non-existent
intermediate steps are of course admissible as long as they are e-
liminated before the final out-put. If mechanical rules are to be
set up for obtaining an out-put, some safe-guard must also be established to avoid results which are completely out of conformity
with the current habits of the speakers of the language. The notion of 'ungrammaticality' serves to establish such a safe-guard,
though with less absolute validity than has been claimed for it.
Even the concentration of attention on writing has, within the limits mentioned in section Id, a certain utility.

III. DANGERS OF FICTIONS

Yet each of these fictions, if its essentially unrealistic and
ad hoc nature is disregarded, can lead to serious error. Neither
the IA nor the IP models, nor even the synchronic approach as a
whole, corresponds completely to reality.[14] It is a commonplace in
scientific discussion to point out that it is impossible for any
observer even to perceive, to say nothing of formulating, the total
state of affairs in any respect at a given point of time.[15] Change
is continually taking place, even while the process of observation

is going on, and hence any formulation of a situation 'as if' it were completely static is fore-doomed to at least a certain inherent inaccuracy, despite its manifest usefulness in many ways. (The parallel with maps and guide-books is valid here, too; the publisher of a map of Hamburg, Germany, states that some change in the city's street- and transport-system, which are represented 'as if' unchanging on his map, takes place on the average once every two days.) The IP fiction has, in itself, no inherent superiority over the IA fiction, as both are simply ways of formulating a synchronic set of relationships which is itself rather fictitious. From one point of view, a clear picture of the IA relationships is essential as a preliminary set of data on which an IP formulation can be set up. In other words, a transformational grammar has to depend on prior analysis of a non-transformational kind. Just as a guide-book depends on previously prepared maps and other types of description, so does transformational grammar draw its data from more fundamental information already gathered concerning a language. A transformational grammar can only be an end-formulation, not an analysis in its own right. If we do not recognize this, we run the risk of concluding that transformational grammar is, in some way, more meritorious in the absolute or more fundamental than other types of linguistic description.

Unidirectionality is, in some respects, useful procedurally; but it implies an *a priori* choice of direction which, if not recognized as imposed by a fiction, is likely to result in an unrecognized transfer of apriorism from procedure to underlying assumptions. This has already taken place in such unwarranted aprioristic statements as that the human ability to acquire language must be explained by a theory of universal general grammar,[16] or that dialect-geography should study language as its users 'ought' to speak, not as they actually do.[17] Such apriorism reaches a point of maximum intensity in postulating that certain aspects of 'mental' activity will forever remain unobservable, and yet must be set up to account for human speech-behavior.[18] It is irrelevant whether these presumed 'mental' factors be considered physical or non-physical. The crucial point is the aprioristic assumption of their permanent unobservability and hence unaccountability. This brings us straight back to Neo-Platonism and the 'idealistic' dualism which has been so harmful, e.g. in the Romance field since Croce and Vossler.[19]

The tendency towards 'either-or' solutions of problems is, according to some observers,[20] very deep-rooted in our culture, and if we do not recognize the fictitious nature of arbitrarily imposed binary choices in linguistic and other analysis, they are lilely to be naively taken as confirmations of already existing biases. This is particularly true of the relation between the notion of 'ungrammaticality' and the purism which we have inherited from Renaissance and Counter-Reformation times. No combination can, in the absolute, be called permanently 'ungrammatical', for new combinations, even of a type which runs most strongly counter to our feeling of 'grammaticality', are always appearing (my most recent example is the sentence *A Record Hunter gift is an always thing*).[21] Many puristic rules, even those of the most mistaken and out-worn kind, are based on transformational principles, e.g. the dogma that one must never say or write *he is better than me*, because *than* is supposedly a con-junction, and that the only 'correct' construction is *he is better than I*, derived by ellipsis ('deletion') from *he is better than I am*.[22] Puristically inclined grammarians are already looking to transformational grammar for support of their dogmatic assertions of 'right' versus 'wrong' in this and similar matters, without rea-lizing the fictional nature of the absolute binary choice involved.[23]

Similarly, the over-concentration of attention on writing has been regarded by some reactionaries as supporting their claims that writing is equal or superior in importance to speech, in the abso-lute. The two major enemies against which linguistics has been pitted ever since the sixteenth century have been our culture's o-ver-emphasis on writing and under-emphasis on speech as the primary aspect of human linguistic behavior,[24] and our puristic tradition, inherited from mediaeval social prejudice, Renaissance classicistic absolutism, and seventeenth-century authoritarianism.[25] We should be careful that no support be afforded by any branch of linguistics to puristic reactionaries, who are still as hostile to our science as ever and are actively working against it.[26]

IV. OTHER DANGERS

There are other aspects of transformational grammar to which objection has frequently been made, and which depend, not on 'as if'-type fictions, but simply on misapprehensions of fact. Among these are the claim that transformational grammar does not make use of meaning, and the frequent assumption that the kernel structure of SUBJECT + PREDICATE must be the same for all languages (as when, say, Italian *névica* or Spanish *nieva* or Latin *ninguit* 'it snows" is treated as having, of necessity, a zeroed-out subject. The former notion is simply a special case of the general belief that any type of linguistic analysis can or should be carried on without re-ference to meaning — an approach which should long since have been exorcised by the well-balanced observations of such scholars as L. Bloomfield and C. C. Fries.[27] The second-mentioned misapprehension is, as has already been pointed out,[28] an unwarranted transfer of English and French structure to other languages of different build: in the conervative Romance languages and in Latin, for instance, the kernel major-clause-type is PREDICATE = VERB alone, and the subject is simply an optional amplification of the person-and-num-ber-reference inherent in the finite verb. There is the risk, at present, that transformational grammar, if based primarily on Eng-lish, may impose on linguistic description an Anglicizing strait-jacket fully as distorting as the Latinizing one of traditional Re-naissance grammar. To avoid such distortions, the application of transformational techniques to the statement of Romance and other

languages will have to be done in terms of the structure of those
languages themselves, and the approach of the transformational
grammarian will have to be more adaptable than it has been here-
tofore.

V. CONCLUSION

Transformational grammar is, it seems to me, neither a new be-
all-and-end-all for linguistics, nor a completely wrong-headed and
objectionable heresy. Mankind's linguistic behavior is too complex
to be completely summed up in any set of mere rules, no matter how
extensive; but transformational grammar can be very useful in certain types of linguistic description and of applied linguistics, as
long as it is kept in proper perspective. Some, though not all,
relations among linguistic elements can be stated conveniently in
terms of transformational processes, especially those involving ze-
roing-out (e.g. Italian *un merci* [m.sg.] 'a goods-train' ← *un treno*
[m.sg.] *merci* [f.pl.]); yet a purely transformational grammar is as
artificial a product as a purely static IA grammar. The most effi-
cient type of description will combine the two in an eclectic approach (not even shunning the use of the old-fashioned paradigmatic
statement where this is most economical).[29] In some situations
(e.g. programmed learning) where a single-step-by-single-step presentation is necessary, transformational techniques may be helpful.
They are also useful in contributing to the design of more conventional language-learning text-books, especially in the preparation
of pattern-drills, if they are not allowed to dictate the entire
structure of the book (a procedure which is disastrous to usefulness of content and maintenance of student-interest).[30]

On the other hand, if the 'as-if' fictions which we have just
described are not recognized as such, and if the other erroneous
notions mentioned in Section IV are allowed to persist, there is
the ever-present danger that transformational or other types of ul-
tra-structured grammar will lose touch with linguistic reality,
which is that of individual humans speaking to and responding to
the speech of other individual humans in the context of their social relationships. In this case, it becomes a mere skating-around
on the surface ice of linguistic structure and the cutting, as it
were, of fancy figures for their own sake — in other words, simply
another type of degeneration of linguistic analysis into empty jugglery. Needless to say, the position I have taken in this paper is
that such a degeneration need not take place, and that transformational grammar, if kept within bounds, can prove and has proven to
be a useful addition to the techniques of linguistic description.[31]

NOTES

1.   Vaihinger (1924); cf. also Hill (1962a)
2.   Vaihinger (1924:109-124).
3.   As discussed especially by Chomsky(1967b) and Lees (1957,
1960), and summarized by Bach (1964). For the most cogent recent

criticism of transformational grammar from the view-point of general linguistics, cf. Uhlenbeck (1963).
    4.   Cf. Hockett (1954).
    5.   As pointed out by Bolinger (1960a).
    6.   Exemplified in such descriptions as that of Oneida in
Lounsbury (1953); cf. my review thereof in Hall (1954).
    7.   E.g. the sketches in Boas (ed.) (1911-1935); Haas (1941);
Newman (1944); or Hall (1948a, 1948b).
    8.   It is widely thought that transformational grammar has de-
veloped to a considerable extent in the course of research in machine-translation (e.g. Joos [1961:20]). This has been explicitly
denied by A. N. Chomsky and others; nevertheless, the relation between machine-translation and transformational grammar is quite
close, and the wide-spread popularity and use of the latter has
obviously been determined in large measure by the vogue of the former and of mathematic approaches to linguistic in general (as
pointed out, for instance, by Garvin [1963]).
    9.   Lees (1960:102).
    10. E.g. Hill (1961).
    11. Lees (1960:121-122).
    12. E.g. Halle (1962); Stockwell (1960). Cf. the remarks of
Householder (1965).
    13. Cf. most recently the discussion by Edfeldt (1960).
    14. Failure to recognize this fact has led to much useless,
sterile discussion, especially among the followers of F. de Saussure, concerning the interrelation of the synchronic and the diachronic axes.
    15. Eddington (1958: ch. 2).
    16. Chomsky (1962:529 ff.).
    17. Chomsky (1964a).
    18. E.g. the statements of M. Halle concerning phonology dis-
cussed by Hill (1962a); Katz (1964).
    19. Cf. Hall (1963).
    20. E.g. E. T. Hall (1963:65-66).
    21. Advertisement in the *New York Times* (records-section), De-
cember 22, 1963. This advertising-slogan is, it seems, a variation
on the title of a song 'Love is a some-times thing'; but the main
point of my observation remains the same.
    22. In fact, *than* is a preposition in modern English, as shown
unequivocally by relative constructions like *Senator Jumbo, than
whom there is no greater wind-bag*. Of course, the formulation of
the function of *than* as a preposition rather than a conjunction can
be perfectly easily taken care of in a transformational grammar, by
the appropriate rule-juggling; but my point is here that tradition-
alist grammarians are already making an unjustified appeal to certain surface similarities between their methods and those of traditional grammar.
    23. For a good instance of explicit defence of traditional Lat-
inizing grammar on the part of machine-translation-oriented transformationalists, cf Pilch (1963). To school-teachers, Lees (1963)
holds out the prospect that transformational grammar will free them
from the necessity of 'complicated' phonemic transcriptions (again

the emphasis on writing over against speech, and an appeal to inertia).

24.   This is not to deny the importance of writing in our culture, or the possibility that in some fields (e.g. mathematics), writing can indicate some things that speech cannot (cf. Hockett [1958: ch. 6]). Recognition of these facts does not, however, justify us in making any concession concerning the basic priority of linguistic structure (including speech) over writing as a whole.

25.   Cf. my discussion in Hall (1950a; 1964: ch. 62).

26.   As shown most recently in the viciously unprincipled attacks on the third edition of Webster's *New International Dictionary* (cf. Dykema [1963]).

27.   Bloomfield (1933a, passim); Fries (1954, 1961).

28.   E.g. in the review of Chomsky (1957a) by Francescato (1958).

29.   As pointed out, for instance, by Gleason (1955 [1961²]: 217).

30.   As it is, for instance, in Roberts et al. (1963).

31.   My position is, therefore, essentially the same as that of Sobelman (1964:260).

SOME RECENT STUDIES
ON PORT-ROYAL AND VAUGELAS

(Acta Linguistica Hafniensia 12.207-233 [1970])

The *Grammaire universelle et raisonnée* or "Grammaire de Port-Royal" of Claude Lancelot and Antoine Arnauld (first published in 1660; third, definitive edition, 1676) has undergone several fluctuations in critical esteem. On its first appearance, and for nearly two centuries thereafter, it enjoyed great popularity, going through five editions and fifteen reprints up to 1846.[1] It is widely recognized[2] that Port-Royal was a prime source of the "universal grammar" movement of the eighteenth century, influencing such theoreticians as du Marsais,[3] Beauzée, Destutt de Tracy, Court de Gébelin, etc., down to Girault-Duvivier.[4] In the nineteenth and early twentieth century, especially under the influence of historical linguistics with a scientific (i.e. monistic, objectivist) orientation,[5] Port-Royal and "universal grammar" fell into disrepute because of their Neo-Platonic dualism, apriorism, frequent neglect or disregard of facts, and lack of historical perspective.[6] More recently, however, with the recrudescence of a dualistic, aprioristic approach and consequent renewed belief in the immediate attainability of a "general" or "universal" grammar, there have been several editions and extensive discussion of Port-Royal, both in itself and in relation to Vaugelas. My purpose here is to sketch briefly the situation prevailing in the 1660's with regard to discussion of language-matters in France; to discuss Arnauld and Lancelot's grammar itself; and to evaluate some recent publications dealing with Port-Royal and Vaugelas.

1. THE BACKGROUND. The four leading language-specialists of the mid-seventeenth century were Claude Favre de Vaugelas (1595-1650), Antoine Arnauld (1612-1694) and his collaborator Claude Lancelot (1615-1695), and Gilles Ménage (1615-1692). Of these, Vaugelas, belonging to an earlier generation than the other three, was the first to deal with problems of French, in his *Remarques sur la langue française* (1st ed., 1648).[7] Lancelot was a successful teacher of the classical languages,[8] and had published widely used "methods" for Latin (in 1644), Greek (in 1655), and Italian (in 1659). Arnauld's concern was with philosophy and logic rather than with grammar in the narrow sense of language-teaching, but his collaboration with Lancelot was the source of the Port-Royal grammar.[9] His closely related *Logique* (1662) was written in collaboration with Pierre Nicole. Ménage's interest lay primarily in the historical field; his chief linguistic works were the *Dictionnaire étymologique ou Origines de la langue française* (1650), *Origini della lingua italiana* (1669), and *Observations sur la langue française* (1672-76).

In general, both in their own time and later, Vaugelas and
Port-Royal have been regarded as the chief representatives of seventeenth-century French linguistic theory, Ménage being left out of
consideration (see below). The basis on which Vaugelas and the
Messieurs de Port-Royal operated was essentially the same. Their
common approach to language included formulation in terms of rules
rather than of descriptive statements; use of ellipsis as a grammatical technique (cf. Vaugelas' observations on the gender of adjectives in comparisons, *Remarques* 2, pp. 188-189); a belief in
correctness ("good" versus "bad" language), to be imposed by authority; and the recognition of usage as one of these authorities. The
differences between them sprang mainly from their divergent aims.
Vaugelas was a courtier, and his *Remarques* were intended, as he expressly stated,[10] to aid speakers in conforming to the language-habits of the court. For this purpose, he rightly regarded current
usage as the only authority, without regard to its rationality or
otherwise. We must emphasize that he was treating almost exclusively of spoken, not literary or philosophical, French, and only of
the situation at court. He therefore ascribed to authors and the
haute bourgeoisie a lower standing than the court, granting the
former only a certain authority in conferring, as it were, a seal
of approval on the latter's usage. Vaugelas was comparable to,
say, Henry W. Fowler, Bergen and Cornelia Evans, or Alfredo Panzini[11] in modern times, as a recorder and promulgator of usage to
be recommended or condemned.

Arnauld and Lancelot, on the other hand, were not aiming at
recommendations for usage, except as a by-product of their efforts
to explain language in terms of logic and reason. It has long been
recognized[12] that Cartesian rationalism played a dominant rôle in
Arnauld's out-look on logic and hence on grammar. Hence the Messieurs de Port-Royal inevitably take "la raison," in the seventeenth-century sense, as their main guide-line in evaluating linguistic phenomena. Usage, for them, was to be dominant only in
those aspects of language which were inexplicable by reason.[13] On
occasion, as in their well-known discussion of the use of a relative clause to modify only an antecedent having a definite article
(*Gr. Gén.* II, ch. 10), they would criticize Vaugelas (not always
successfully; cf. below), to explain by reason what he had observed
in usage. We must not conclude from this, however, that Arnauld
and Lancelot were diametrically opposed to Vaugelas. Rather, starting from largely identical premisses, they went off in a different
direction, that of Cartesian logicism and rationalism, and natural-
ly reached different conclusions from those of Vaugelas.

In contrast to both Vaugelas (whose basic approach was synchronic) and Port-Royal (whose logicism aimed at being achronic, but
was actually synchronic),[14] Ménage had a diachronic approach, with
a time-perspective of two millennia. In his extensive knowledge of
Old French literature,[15] he was a *rara avis* among seventeenth-century Frenchmen. In his work on French and Italian etymology, Ménage continued directly the traditions established in the previous

century by Claudio Tolomei and Celso Cittadini,   but unfortunately without the former's methodological insight.[17] As Turgot expressly recognized a hundred years later,[18] seventeenth- and eighteenth-century historians of language had no guide-line with regard to phonetic development. Such a guide-line, the principle of regularity in sound-change, had indeed been discovered by Tolomei but was forgotten in the Baroque period, and was not rediscovered until the nineteenth century. To his interest in historical linguistics, Ménage added a strong predilection for society-life, so that his philogical divagations became well known in non-intellectual circles [19] Most of Ménage's etymologies were right,[20] but he admitted such random, in fact wild phonetic developments that some of them were, even to the untrained eye, ridiculous. His derivations of Fr. *haricot* < *faba* and of It. *alfana* 'steed' < *equus* became notorious.[21] Such free-wheeling treatment of word-history contributed greatly to the disesteem in which etymology was held until it received a solid, scientific base in the nineteenth century. Ménage's 28% of wrong etymologies thus outweighed, in the eyes of his own and later generations, his 72% of right ones, so that even today he is badly underestimated in the history of linguistics.[22]

2. THE *Grammaire générale et raisonnée*. The Port-Royal *Grammaire* consists of two markedly uneven parts, one dealing with sounds and their written representation ("Première Partie, où il est parlé des lettres & des caractères de l'écriture", pp. 6-25),[23] and the other with forms and their use ("Seconde Partie, où il est parlé des principes & des raisons sur lesquelles sont appuyées les diverses formes et la signification des mots" (pp. 26-161). The second part is organized primarily according to the various parts of speech, beginning with substantives[24] (pp. 30-51) and proceeding to articles (pp. 51-58), pronouns (pp. 59-87), prepositions (pp. 88-92), and adverbs (pp. 93-94). Most of the remainder of the second part is devoted to the verb (pp. 94-150; this is followed by short chapters on conjunctions and interjections (pp. 150-153) and on syntax (pp. 153-160). The order in which the parts of speech are presented reflects Arnauld's and Lancelot's view of their function, in which substantives (and their determiners), pronouns, prepositions, and adverbs denote the objects of our thoughts, and verbs, conjunctions, and interjections denote the form and manner thereof (pp. 29-30). The content of the *Grammaire* is analysed extensively by both Miss Sahlin and Donzé (see below). Here, we shall discuss briefly only certain aspects of Port-Royal's approach which are particularly relevant to recent discussions: the implications of the title, especially of the two adjectives *generale* and *raisonnée*; and the presuppositions underlying the analytical procedures of the Messieurs de Port-Royal.

Not only from the title, but also from other indications in the text, the reader is conditioned to expect Arnauld and Lancelot's observations and doctrines to have universal applicability. The term *toutes les langues*, for which one or another statement is declared to be valid, occurs eleven times throughout the work. Yet

the languages from which examples are drawn are only seven (given
here with the total number of points in connection with which each
is cited:[25] French (106), Latin (84), Greek (35), Hebrew (22), Italian and Spanish (5 each), and German (4); plus three language-
groups, all of them rather ill-defined:[26] "les langues vulgaires"
(15), "les langues orientales" (3) and "les langues du Nord" (1).
In comparison with preceding discussions of language, this list
does indeed represent a considerable broadening of the horizon; but
it is still limited to the Indo-European family, with the sole ex=
ception of Hebrew and "Oriental" languages (whatever they may have
been). There are many points for which universality is claimed,
which investigation of other language-families has disproved, such
as the statement (p. 155) that every nominative must always imply
some verb "understood" or "deleted". The Messieurs de Port-Royal
needed only to examine more closely some of the languages with
which they dealt to see the inaccuracy of some of their claims,
e.g. the notion (pp. 155-156) that every verb implies a nominative expressed or understood (the Latin impersonals such as *pluit*,
tonat are cases in point).[27] To the same type of glottocentrism
belongs their concept of "natural" word-order (II, ch. 6 and elsewhere). One wonders where they got the information that all languages necessarily have a schwa (I, ch.2). For the languages with
which seventeenth-century French philosophers, grammarians and teachers usually dealt, many of Arnauld and Lancelot's statements do
have a fairly wide applicability. Three hundred years later, however, when our horizon has widened to include well over a thousand
of the world's languages, a book using only French and Latin for
over two-thirds of its exemplifications can hardly be considered
to have anything resembling universal or even general validity.[28]

From the adjective *raisonnée* in the title, and the continual
reference to *la raison* (especially as opposed to irrational "usage") in the book, it has normally been argued that the Port-Royal
grammar represents the application of Descartes' principles to linguistic analysis.[29] There are many definitions of "reason" in the
abstract; one of the best, especially in relation to science, is
that given by MacMurray (1935:19-22):

> Reason is the capacity to behave, not in terms of our
> own nature, but in terms of our knowledge of the nature
> of the world outside. [...] Reason is thus our capaci-
> ty for objectivity. [...] Science rests upon the de-
> sire to know things in their objective nature. [...]
> Where objective knowledge fails we can only act subjec-
> tively, on impulse. It is thus the effort to create the
> conditions of rational activity that gives rise to sci-
> ence. [...] Reason demands that our beliefs should
> conform to the nature of the world, not to the nature of
> our hopes and ideals.

The type of rational, objective, and hence scientific investigation envisaged by MacMurray can be achieved by the four steps

which Descartes set up for himself in the *Discours de la méthode* (ch. II), if taken all together and in the proper order: (1) use of only verified data; (2) analysis into the smallest possible units (*parcelles*); (3) synthesis, proceeding from the simple to the complex; (4) review.

However, the normal seventeenth-century view of *la raison*, as equivalent to *le bon sens* (which latter was, according to Descartes himself, "la chose la mieux partagée du monde") was considerably more ethnocentric and culturally conditioned. In language-matters, especially, ever since the time of the Modistae,[30] philosophers had equated "reason" and "logic" with the analysis of the *modi significandi* — which, in their turn, were directly (though unacknowledgedly) based on the categories of Latin as set up by Priscian and other grammarians. The Messieurs de Port-Royal combined the approach of mediaeval speculative grammarians[31] with part, but not all, of Cartesian method. Arnauld and Lancelot assume *a priori* that the facts of grammar are already well established, so that they need not be discovered, but only presented. That is to say, Port-Royal puts into practice only the third step of Descartes' procedure. [32] Their approach is therefore only partly Cartesian, since their neglect of his first two steps results in an aprioristic, nonscientific attitude.[33] They are rationalistic only in the mediaeval sense of the term, in which logic and reason are defined, not by objectivity, but by adherence to analytical categories predetermined (largely outside of the logician's awareness) by those of Latin grammar.[34]

At the out-set of Part II (ch. 1), Arnauld and Lancelot state that, having treated the material side of language, they are now passung to its spiritual aspect ("il nous reste à considérer ce qu'elle [sc. la parole] a de spirituel" (p. 27). The title of this chapter is "Que la connaissance de ce qui se passe dans notre esprit, est nécessaire pour comprendre les fondemens de la Grammaire; & que c'est de là que dépend la diversité des mots qui composent le discours" (p. 26). The rest of the book contains numerous references to "les mouvemens de l'esprit" and "ce qui se passe dans notre esprit". This approach to language was of course a reflection of the all-pervasive mind-versus-matter dualism which seventeenth-century European thought had inherited from mediaeval theology and Renaissance Neo-Platonism.[35] No matter which side of the current debates over mentalism and objectivism one is on, it still must be admitted that the only way to attain "la connaissance de ce qui se passe dans notre esprit" is through an analysis of what we say and what it means; and that there is, therefore, in any dualistic approach to language an inevitable circularity, whether we consider it praise-worthy or not.

The Messieurs de Port-Royal share with virtually all other grammarians of the Middle Ages, Renaissance, and Baroque period a non-historical, static approach to language-phenomena. Their actual references to earlier stages of French in the *Grammaire universelle* are very few, and such statements as they do make are

normally wrong. Thus, in accounting for exceptions to their rule
that relative clauses always modify a noun with some kind of determiner (II, ch. 10), they say:

> S'il y a d'autres façons de parler qui y sont con-
> traires, dont on ne puisse rendre raison par toutes ces
> observations, ce ne pourront estre, comme je le croy,
> que des restes du vieux stile, où on omettait presque
> toujours les articles.

In actuality, Old French usage with regard to the articles was
far more complicated than mere "omission" almost all the time.
Their observations on the absence of agreement with certain present
participles (e.g. *j'ay vue une femme lisant l'Escriture* [p. 112])
might have been improved had they known anything of the invariabil-
ity of the present participle in Old French.[37] Ménage could have
told them better, but there is no reference to him in Port-Royal.
Beyond their neglect of such linguistic history as was known at the
time, however, their entire philosophy of language rests on the
assumption that the world and human life are static. This is especially apparent in their adoption (through mediaeval scholastic
channels[38]) of the Aristotelian doctrine that every verb can be
interpreted as equivalent to *be* + a present participle (as in
affirmat = est affirmans; *Pierre vit = Pierre est vivant*, etc. [pp.
100-101). Thus, mere existence, as indicated by the verb *be*, is
elevated to a fundamental rôle in all human affirmation, and all
activities are relegated to the function of attributes. Such a
view is wholly consonant with the static, absolutist, authoritarian out-look of the French Baroque;[39] it is quite contrary to the
Humboldtian conception of language as an *energeia*, an activity,
rather than as an *ergon* or non-living, unchanging thing (to say nothing of Faust's *Im Anfang war die Tat!*).

Even with regard to the facts of the languages they were discussing, Arnauld and Lancelot were often wrong. Previous commen-
tators have remarked this with regard to the Port-Royal treatment
of the relative clause modifying a noun (pp. 79-88),[40] of the impersonal verbs (pp. 125-130),[41] of the presumed tripartite nature
of the clause-proposition,[42] and of the agreement of past participles in perfect-phrases.[43] Their attempt to discuss French impersonals in relation to Italian is particularly naïve,[44] and the Italian phrase which they cite (p. 129), **il caldo fa* 'it is hot', is
simply not possible in Italian. If "descriptive adequacy" is to be
a criterion for judging grammars,[45] Port-Royal falls down rather
badly on more than one count.

The fore-going criticisms are not meant to give the impression
that the Port-Royal grammar has no merits at all. It is a reasonably solid, fairly traditional presentation of the main features of
Latin grammar, in particular of the parts of speech and their meanings. It would hardly be possible to extract a satisfactory French
grammar from the Port-Royal work, but it does contain a number of

improvements over previous descriptions of the French language.[46]
Their treatment of the definite and indefinite article was far superior to that given by previous grammarians, and they hit the
bull's-eye in their definition of the function of the verb — i.e.
the meaning of the form-class — in Latin and French (which can be
extended to other Indo-European languages) as "affirmation" (II,
ch. 13.).[47] But it has been necessary to emphasize the shortcomings
of the Port-Royal grammar to make clear how short it falls, with
regard not only to modern standards for the presentation of linguistic phenomena, but also of the complete sequence of steps
which Descartes set up for scientific analysis and a rational procedure. Port Royal's grammar is, from this point of view, only
partly Cartesian and, instead of being truly rational and hence
scientific, is only rationalistic.

3. BREKLE'S EDITION AND ARTICLES. Brekle's 1966 edition consists officially of two volumes. The single book which the reader
holds in his hand, however, is Tome I, and Tome II is simply a pa-
per-bound pamphlet which fits into a cloth pocket in the inside
back cover of the binding of the first volume. Vol. I contains the
main body of the book: Brekle's prefatory material (pp. v-xxxii),
a facsimile reprint of the 166 pages of the third edition (1676) of
the *Grammaire générale*, and a table of contents of the whole volume. The front-matter includes a brief preface (pp. v-vi), a section on "La *Grammaire générale* hier et aujourd'hui" (pp. vii-xiii),
"Les deux auteurs de la *Grammaire générale*" (pp. xiv-xv), an exposition of the development of the text (pp. xvi-xvii), "Critères a-
doptés pour cette édition critique" (pp. xvii-xviii), and an extensive bibliography of (1a) the editions of the *Grammaire générale*
from 1610 to 1846 (pp. xviii-xx), (1b) translations (pp. xxi-xxiii)
and (II) works bearing on the book and its authors (pp. xxiv-
xxxii). The second "volume" lists the variants between the editions of 1660 and 1676/79; a few "Remarques sur les variations"
(p. 7) are folllowed by a list (pp. 9-37) of the variants themselves, in two columns (1660 on the left, 1676 on the right)), and
a three-column presentation (p. 39) of the chapter-numbers in the
first four editions (1664, 1664, and 1676/79). Brekle's editorial
work has been thorough and careful, so that the Port-Royal grammar
is now easily available in a trust-worthy reprint.

Brekle has discussed the *Grammaire générale* and its position in
the history of linguistics in the Introduction to his 1966 reprint
and in his two articles.[48] His main concern is with the rehabili-
tation of Arnauld and Lancelot as predecessors of certain trends in
current linguistic theory. His 1964 article is concerned primarily
with the semiotic aspect of grammar and logic, as seen by the Messieurs de Port-Royal in their insistence on the close relation between the two; he concludes (p. 121):

> Die vorliegenden Interpretationsergebnisse beweisen,
> dasz die Autoren der 'Grammaire' und 'Logique' die Be-
> deutung einer zeichen- und sprachtheoretischen Fundie-

rung von Aussagen über Sprache und Logik erkannt haben.
Damit treffen sich die Denker und Lehrer von Port-Royal
mit einem modernen wissenschaftlichs-theoretischen
Trend, das für alle Grundlagenwissenschaften eine Re-
flexion auf semiotische und linguistische Voraussetzun-
gen zu implizieren scheint. Von diesem Standpunkt aus
läszt sich ihre denkerische Leistung, von der hier nur
ein Teil angedeutet werden sollte, gerade heute würdi-
gen und verstehen.

In his 1966 article, Brekle is concerned chiefly with tying
Port-Royal in with various modern trends, especially the search
for universals (pp. 3-4). The similarities with Chomskyan transformational doctrines are quite obvious: "deep" versus "surface"
structure (pp. 4-6), and the problem of the universality of case,
whether it is present in a given language or not (cf. our fn. 34).
Similarly, Port-Royal's notorious expansion of *Dieu invisible a
créé le monde visible* into *Dieu qui est invisible a créé le monde
qui est visible* involves the same type of paraphrase of an adjective by a relative clause as does Chomsky's interpretation of noun-
modifiers (pp. 10-14). Brekle interprets Lancelot's discussion as
involving an expansion of this sentence into its "underlying
strings".[49]   (For the validity of this interpretation, see below).
Brekle is broad-minded enough to see in Port-Royal anticipations
of, not only Chomskyan transformationalism, but also "structural"
linguistics, in the definition of the noun as the head of a noun-
phrase and the adjective as modifier thereto (p. 7); in Port-Royal's "signification distincte" equated with Fries's "lexical meaning" (Fries [1954]); and "signification confuse" = Fries's "grammatical meaning" (pp. 9-10), and in the distinction between sex-refe-
rence and grammatical gender (p. 10).

Brekle's enthusiasm for Port-Royal leads him to defend Arnauld
and Lancelot against the condemnation of such critics as Cognet
(pp. vii-ix of his 1966 edition). This commendable zeal sometimes
carries him too far, as when he says (p. xiii):

> Donc, cette oeuvre magistrale ne marque pas seulement
> une date importante dans l'histoire de la langue françai-
> se (comme on l'a jugé dans le passé), mais c'est plutôt
> une des oeuvres qui sont vraiment dignes d'être incluses
> dans le canon des oeuvres linguistiques en la rangeant à
> coté d'un Cours de linguistique générale par F. de Saus-
> sure et des oeuvres écrites par Sapir, Bloomfield, etc.

No: whatever its merits, the Port-Royal grammar is far from being
either broad enough or profound enough in its coverage of human
language as a whole to qualify it for a position alongside any of
these.

4. DONZÉ'S AND OTHER DISCUSSIONS. In her book on Du Marsais,
Miss Sahlin organized each chapter so as to present "Théories avant

la *Grammaire générale*" and "Théories des grammairiens philosophes avant du Marsais", with especial attention to Port-Royal before coming to her main subject. It would be possible to extract from Miss Sahlin's work an extensive compilation of highly intelligent critical discussion of Arnauld and Lancelot. However, Port-Royal was after all not her main subject, and forty years have passed. There was room for a new, thorough, objective discussion centred directly on the *Grammaire générale* itself. Donzé's book[50] fully satisfies this need.

The book consists of three main parts, plus subsidiary material. After an Introduction (pp. 7-21) presenting the back-ground and the relation of the *Grammaire générale* to its authors' other activities, the first part (pp. 25-44) deals with "La méthode de Port-Royal", with two chapters: one on its relation to Descartes (pp. 25-34), especially in Arnauld and Lancelot's definition of the verb; and one on its relation to theories of usage, particularly, of course, those of Vaugelas (pp. 35-44). The second part, "Les mots" (pp. 45-124), is divided into three chapters: "Théorie du signe" (pp. 47-59), "Les parties du discours" (pp. 60-91), and "Théorie des accidents" (i.e. categories of inflection) (pp. 92-124). Part Three, "Les fonctions" (pp. 125-171), contains a brief introduction (pp. 127-128), and three chapters, each with a number of subdivisions: "L'analyse prédicative de la proposition" (pp. 129-136), "La théorie des propositions complexes et composées" (pp. 137-158), and "Syntaxe de convenance et syntaxe de régime" (pp. 159-171). A brief "Conclusion" (pp. 173-179) sums up Donzé's findings and evaluates Arnauld and Lancelot's work in relation to later approaches to languages, especially those of the eighteenth-century "grammairiens philosophes" and of Saussure (pp. 178-179). Copious notes are contained in a separate section (pp. 181-224), followed by an appendix (pp. 225-226) listing the table of contents of the *Grammaire générale* and the chapter-numbers of the 1660 and 1676 editions. A very full bibliography ("Ouvrages de Port-Royal", pp. 227-228; "Grammaires anciennes", pp. 228-230; "Autres ouvrages consultes", pp. 230-235) and two indices ("Auteurs cités", pp. 237-239, and "Notions", pp. 240-253) complete the book.

Donzé's treatment of Arnauld and Lancelot's grammar is outstanding for its thoroughness and its objectivity. He is clearly sympathetic to their work, and analyses it from both a descriptive and a historical point of view. On each point, he expounds their primisses, analytical procedures, and conclusions, with his own answers to possible objections and also his own evaluation of their findings. For instance, in connection with their treatment of the verb and its meaning, he says (pp. 27-28):

Voici comme Arnauld et Lancelot procèdent.

Ils prennent appui sur ce qui a été dit de la proposition, et qu'ils considèrent comme étant démontré dans le chapitre qui introduit la deuxième partie de l'ouvrage.

'La connaissance de la nature du verbe dépend de ce
que nous avons dit au commencement de ce discours:
que le jugement que nous faisons des choses (comme
quand je dis, *la terre est ronde*) enferme nécessaire-
ment deux termes: l'un appelé *sujet*, qui est ce dont
on affirme, comme *terre*; & l'autre appelé *attribut*,
qui est ce dont on affirme, comme *ronde*; & de plus,
la liaison entre ces deux termes, qui est proprement
l'action de notre esprit qui affirme l'attribut du
sujet' (Gr. II, Ch. XIII, p. 49).

Le sujet et l'attribut, en tant qu'ils sont conçus
(et non pas affirmés) sont l'objet de notre pensée;
et la liaison (en tant qu'elle affirme) en est proprement l'action ou la manière; or comme les hommes
ont besoin d'inventer des mots (les noms) qui marquent les objects de leur pensée, ils ont eu encore
besoin d'en créer (les verbes) qui marquent son
action:

'Et c'est proprement ce que c'est que le verbe,
un mot dont le principal usage est de signifier
l'affirmation, c'est-à-dire, de marquer que le discours où ce mot est employé, est le discours d'un
homme qui ne conçoit pas seulement des choses, mais
qui en juge & qui les affirme' (p. 80).

Il s'agit maintenant d'établir (à partir de ces
prémisses) la vérité de la proposition.

He then proceeds to show how they answer such objections as that
nouns also "affirm", or that the imperative and the desiderative
are on the same level as the indicative in affirming. After this,
Donzé passes to their distinction between the verb *to be* as "substantive" when it affirms pure existence, and *to be* or all other
verbs as "adjective" when they indicate further attributes of the
subject beyond that of pure existence.

Like Miss Sahlin, Donzé puts the doctrines of Port-Royal in
historical perspective. He goes somewhat beyond her procedure, by
introducing appropriate comparisons from all periods of linguistics, ranging from the ancient grammarians to Chomsky. He rightly
rejects (pp. 220-221) the last-mentioned's ascription of a transformational interpretation of *Dieu invisible a créé le monde visible*
to Arnauld and Lancelot, pointing out:

Arnauld et Lancelot se réfèrent manifestement ici,
plutôt qu'à une hypothétique psychologie des formes,
à la théorie logique des incidentes considérées comme
le produit d'un jugement antérieur.[51]

Donzé sacrifices, in his evaluation of Port-Royal, none of his in-

tellectual independence; he shows himself quite ready to disagree
with the Messieurs de Port-Royal at many points (a rough count
shows 27 such). He criticizes them on such matters as their continually recurrent imagery of the deliberate invention of language
(p. 50);[52] the division of the parts of speech according to logico-
semantic criteria (pp. 63-66); their theory of nouns (pp. 71-72),
personal pronouns (pp. 79-80), relative pronouns (pp.85-86), gender
(.p99), impersonal verbs (p. 101 and note 77 [pp. 106-107]), voice
(pp. 105, 112), the Latin gerundive (p. 109), moods (pp. 118-119),
the presumed three forms of thought (p. 131), the verb in relation
to the terms of judgement (p. 134), the relation of sentence-
structure thereto (pp. 134-136), and their failure to recognize
agreement as an indicator of dependence (p. 161); their readiness
to equate the study of language with that of the "operations of the
mind" (p. 175); the absurdity of equating the French conjunction
que (Latin *quod*) with the relative pronoun (note 49, pp. 206-207);
and so forth.

In addition to Donzé's book, three relatively recent articles
deal with Port-Royal.[53]   Into the first of these, Port-Royal en-
ters primarily as part of the background of "logicalist" analysis
which Coseriu rightly criticizes. He is wrong, on the other hand, in
the one place where he refers to Arnauld and Lancelot by name (his
fn. 53), where, after criticizing those who confuse lexical meaning
with that of formal categories, he says:

> En cambio, fuerza es recordarlo, no caían en lo mismo
> los campeones del logicismo gramatical, A. Arnauld y
> C. Lancelot, quienes distinguían con mucha agudeza y en
> un sentido aún hoy aceptable, entre función verbal y
> función sustantiva [...].

Foucault's brief article is a rather naïve presentation of Port-Royal's main approach and doctrines, taken *au pied de la lettre*. It
is worth noting, however, that he too perceives the basic identity
of approach to language, in terms of rules, between Port-Royal and
Vaugelas (p. 7). After discussing the former's ideal of a language
as conforming to its "loi intérieure", he remarks (fn. 1):

> On voit ici la différence avec Vaugelas. Toutefois,
> dans la mesure où celui-ci donne l'usage comme critère,
> il pense bien lui aussi la règle comme loi d'existence
> d'une langue.

Chevalier, on the other hand, gives a considerably more extensive critique and evaluation of Port-Royal in relation to modern
linguistics, from Brunot to Chomsky. After discussing (pp. 16-17)
the former's objections to the assumption of wide-spread ellipsis
("supposer une ellipse c'était refuser la vérité des faits") and to
the influence of Latin grammar and aprioristic philosophical considerations, Chevalier passes rapidly over the unfruitful treatments
given by Harnois (1928) and others, and then notes the later revi-

val of interest, especially on the part of Chomsky (1966). He discusses and criticizes Foucault's appreciation of Port-Royal (pp.
17-19), Chomsky's book (pp. 19-22), and Snyders' treatment of its
pedagogical aspect[54] (pp. 22-32). Chevalier is especially right
in emphasizing the pedagogical side of Lancelot's work. Too often,
the *Grammaire générale* is treated as if it were a purely abstract,
philosophical treatise, instead of a school-book intended primarily
to present the fundamental notions of Latin and French grammar for
learners on the intermediate level. In his conclusion (pp. 32-33),
Chevalier points out the way in which Port-Royal subordinates the
study of actual linguistic manifestations to that of "la proposition, cadre unique auquel on ramène tous les autres, puisqu'il est
tenu pour le schéma nécessaire du raisonnement" (p. 32), and then
observes "Un outil remarquable par son abstraction est donc offert
à une élite pour la réduction à l'unité d'un monde désordonné" (p.
33). (Note the social implications of this remark!) In his final
paragraph, Chevalier comments on what, after all, could hardly es-
cape any unprejudiced observer:

> Si la *Grammaire* de Port-Royal a eu l'inappréciable mé-
> rite de donner son relief à la grammaire, de décoller la
> Syntaxe du monde des signes formels, elle, à l'inverse,
> écrase les efforts des grammairiens formels pour établir
> la spécificité de chaque langue: que le français est
> fondé sur un jeu d'opérateurs tandis que le latin agglu-
> tine des déclinations pour constituer des groupements
> fonctionnels restés à l'arrière-plan. On est passé trop
> vite au domaine de l'universel. C'est à mon avis la le-
> çon qu'en doit tirer la linguistique moderne.[55]

Since Cognet's biography (1950), Vaugelas has received relatively little attention, apart from his relation to Port-Royal. The
only serious discussion has been Mok's article on "Vaugelas et la
désambigüisation de la parole".[56] His main argument is that Vaugelas was but little concerned with ambiguities that might arise from
either phonological similarity (homonymy) or lexical polysemy —
presumably something which simply could not be avoided. For Mok,
Vaugelas was concerned primarily with semantic ambiguity, which he
sought to obviate by distinguishing the different meanings of various structural combinations.

    5. CHOMSKY'S *Cartesian Linguistics*. Except for Miss Sahlin's
discussion of Port-Royal (insofar as Arnauld and Lancelot were predecessors of Du Marsais), the works we have considered so far centre their discussion fairly closely on the *Grammaire générale*.
Chomsky's book[57] covers a much wider range, both in the time-span
covered (primarily from Port-Royal to Humboldt or nearly three centuries) and in the extent of linguistic theory discussed. The book
contains, after some brief front-matter, four main sections (not
chapters, since they do not start on separate pages): "Creative aspect of language use" (pp. 3-31); "Deep and surface structure" (pp.
31-51); "Description and explanation in linguistics" (pp. 52-59);

and "Acquisition and use of language" (pp. 59-73). Extensive notes (pp. 75-112) are followed by a bibliography (pp. 113-119). There is no index.

We have already mentioned Descartes' four steps in scientific analysis. Chomsky's work falls short of meeting the requirements of any one of these. He states (p. 2):

> My primary aim is simply to bring to the attention of those involved in the study of generative grammar and its implications some of the little-known work which has bearing on their concerns and problems and which often anticipates some of their specific conclusions.

However, in so doing, he (1) neglects to give an adequate account of the works which he is discussing or of the back-ground out of which they grew; (2) fails to analyse their content completely; (3) presents their content from a thoroughly biased point of view;[58] and (4) has clearly failed to review the validity of his discussion in relation to other scholars' findings.

In his first section, Chomsky makes much of "creativity" in human use of language, concluding (p. 29):

> In summary, one fundamental contribution of what we have been calling "Cartesian linguistics" is the observation that human language, in its natural use, is free from the control of independently identifiable external stimuli or internal states and is not restricted to any practical communicative function, in contrast, for example, to the pseudo-language of animals. It is thus free to serve as an instrument of free thought and self-expression. The limitless possibilities of thought and imagination are reflected in the creative aspect of language use. The language provides finite means but infinite possibilities of expression constrained only by rules of concept formation and of sentence formation, these being in part particular and idiosyncratic but in part universal, a common human endowment. The finitely specifiable form of each language — in modern terms, its generative grammar [...] — provides an "organic unity" interrelating its basic elements and underlying each of its individual manifestations, which are potentially infinite in number.

Here, as throughout, we have a projection backwards of his own approach onto the views of an earlier period, distorting and misinterpreting them to fit into the Procrustean bed of his frame-work. This is largely shadow-boxing with modern opponents,[59] particularly with Skinnerian behaviorism as he misconceives it.[60] There is a latent polysemy in the term CREATIVE which (as in his use of other terms)[61] Chomsky exploits tacitly. As I have pointed out elsewhere,[62] there has been no such thing as creation in modern man's use of language, for at least the last ten or twenty thousand years, possibly more. No new elements have been introduced into the structure of human languages (e.g. use of previously unexploited parts of the human organism, introduction of hitherto completely unknown types of sounds, categories of form or meaning, etc.). An unlimited number of novel utterances is of course possible, but novelty is not creativity. As the late G. Herdan pointed out,[63] Chomsky neglects the most elementary statistical considerations in seeing something strange and wonderful in the production of an infinite number of combinations from a finite number of elements.

Chomsky cites a number of passages from writers of this period to demonstrate what every-one knows already, that they set up a dualism between mind and matter (inherited from ancient and mediaeval philosophy) and concludes (pp. 29-30):

> The dominant view throughout this period is that "Les langues sont le meilleur miroir de l'esprit humain". This virtual identification of linguistic and mental processes is what motivates the Cartesian test for the existence of other minds, discussed above. It finds expression throughout the romantic period. For Friedrich Schlegel, "so unzertrennlich ist Geist und Sprache, so wesentlich Eins Gedanke und Wort, dasz wir, so gewiss wir den Gedanken als das eigentümliche Vorrecht des Menschen betrachten, auch das Wort, nach seiner innern Bedeutung und Würde als das ursprüngliche Wesen des Menschen nennen können". We have already made reference to Humboldt's conclusion that the force that generates language is indistinguishable from that which generates thought. Echoes of this conclusion persist for some time but they become less frequent as we enter the modern period.

(Luckily for the modern period, one feels tempted to add.) Seriously, though, this passage reflects fully Chomsky's apriorism and his neglect of everything that has been discussed concerning human language since the period he is discussing.[64] Of course, if we start out by deciding in advance that what goes on inside of people's heads (which, to date, has remained inaccessible to direct observation) is identical to what they say, then of course language and "thought", as defined in this wise, are identical. But there is no proof for this assumption. Descartes had none, nor had anyone before or after him. There was nothing especially original in his having made such an assumption, nor did his making it have any real bearing on the validity of his scientific method. Descartes' and others' "mentalism" is, in this connection, simply a red herring dragged across the road leading to objective study of language and other human activities. There is also a covert emotional ap-

peal involved here, to the widely and tenaciously held belief in
the necessary existence of a non-material, permanently inaccessible "spirit", "soul", etc., which is at the base of the distinction between *Geistes-* and *Naturwissenschaften*.[65]

A covert emotional appeal is also involved in the Chomskyan
distinction between "deep" and "surface" structure, which he likewise projects backwards onto Port-Royal.[66] We have already mentioned Donzé's criticisms of Chomsky's interpretation of the NOUN
+ ADJECTIVE construction and of the declarative verb as equivalent
to *be* + PRESENT PARTICIPLE; any objective scholar, looking at the
Port-Royal grammar, could see the short-comings of this approach.
Chomsky, however, forces their interpretation into the frame-work
of his pet distinction between "deep" and "surface" structure (pp.
40-46). Quite aside from the very existence of such a distinction
— whose validity is quite doubtful[67] — it is *antistorico*, as the
Italians would say, to treat either Port-Royal or their successors,
the *grammairiens philosophes*, as in any meaningful way anticipating
this distinction. The only way to do so is to equate "deep structure" with their concept of "les mouvemens de l'esprit" — which
is tantamount to removing "deep structure" from any possibility of
objective and hence scientifically valid observation or discussion.
Here, too, Chomsky neglects what preceded Port-Royal and the eighteenth century, and hence ascribes to them too much originality,
with regard to possible transformationalist interpretations and especially what Miss Sahlin called Lancelot's "mania" (cf. our fn.
49) for tracing all sentences back to one common syntactic kernel.
He lists her book on Du Marsais in his bibliography; even a rapid
glance at her discussion of this point would have shown that Sanctius, not Port-Royal, is the source of this particular procedure,
and Mrs. Lakoff (1969) would not have had to discuss this point at
length in her review of Brekle's edition.

One of Chomsky's favorite whipping-boys has been the descriptive approach to language exemplified by the work of the immediately preceding generation of linguists, which it has pleased him to
call (inaccurately) "taxonomic" and to decry as inadequate to "explain" language. To "taxonomic" linguistics he opposes his own
view, which he claims to have greater "explanatory power" because
it "generates" sentences by transforming them from syntactic kernels. This view, which has gained wide-spread currency in the last
decade,[68] is itself unfounded. Chomsky makes matters worse in
Cartesian Linguistics by projecting it, too, back onto a contrast
between Port-Royal and Vaugelas (pp. 54-57), which is without foundation in historical fact (cf. our section 1, above). Vaugelas is
in no wise comparable to Bloomfield or to Harris, Hockett, or any
others of the "neo-Bloomfieldians" whom transformationalists love
to cast slurs on as "mere taxonomists". Vaugelas was a usage-spe-
cialist, with (as suggested above) the same intellectual back-
ground and the same approach to grammatical phenomena as the Messieurs de Port-Royal. I have found, in *Cartesian Linguistics*,no reference at all to Ménage.

Much the same type of apriorism in his own thinking, and projecting of his own theories back onto the earlier period, is evident in Chomsky's last main section, on the acquisition and use of language. That "ideas" were innate, coming to each individual along with his soul when the latter was infused into him at or before birth, was a common-place from antiquity and mediaeval speculation, and was no special discovery of the "grammairiens philosophes". No competent philosopher or psychologist has entertained such notions since the nineteenth century.[69] In fact, it is probably not too much to say that adherence to the "innateness-hypothesis", in the form in which Chomsky revives it, is *prima facie* evidence of incompetence in philosophy, psychology, or linguistics. Of course, the CAPACITY to use language, as each individual develops it in his idiolect, on the basis of what he learns from those around him as he grows up, is innate, genetically determined, and species-specific.[70] But capacity is not the same thing as competence,[71] and Chomsky's entire misunderstanding on this point comes from a (typical) terminological confusion on his part.

One of the basic requirements of scientific procedure is complete objectivity, which implies, among other things, the exclusion from one's analytical procedure, and from the presentation of one's findings, of all factors connected with one's own emotions or viewpoints on on-scientific matters (including religion, politics, social opinions, or other points of purely personal belief).[72] But Chomsky has spoken out against this objectivist point of view,[73] and has not abstained, in *Cartesian Linguistics*, from introducing his own political beliefs. For instance, in his note 51 (pp. 91-93), Chomsky brings in a linguistically irrelevant quotation from Karl Marx, and then passes to Rousseau's equally irrelevant views on society. His note 115 (pp. 110-111) brings in Humboldt's views on the state. From the gratuitous introduction of political views (of whatever color) in this fashion, to the orientation of an entire branch of science (e.g. linguistics) in one particular direction or another, it is only a short step (as evidenced most strongly, in recent decades, in the dominance of Marrism in Soviet scholarship, under political pressure[74]), and only another short step to the imposition of thought-control in the name of one predetermined "truth" or another.[75]

In his "summary" (pp. 70-71), Chomsky makes the apparently disarming statement:

> It is important to bear in mind that the survey that
> has been presented here is a very fragmentary and there-
> fore in some ways a misleading one. Certain major fig-
> ures — Kant, for example — have not been mentioned or
> have been inadequately discussed, and a certain distor-
> tion is introduced by the organization of the survey,
> as a projection backwards of certain ideas of contempo-
> rary interest rather than as a systematic presentation
> of the framework within which these ideas arose and found

their place.

Well, then — the reader is tempted to ask — if Chomsky's discussion is (by his own admission) so fragmentary, misleading, and distorted, why did he dare to publish it? Protests against the misrepresentations given in *Cartesian Linguistics* have already been made;[76] unfortunately, most of the reviews of the book have been naïvely laudatory,[77] with little realization that Chomsky's disavowals quoted above are actually understatements. A comparison of Chomsky with Donzé shows immediately that, whereas the latter is calm, thorough, objective, and sympathetic but independent-minded enough to remain critical, the former manifests the exact opposite of all these qualities. *Cartesian Linguistics* is incomplete, biased, *antistorico*, and antiscientific; it grossly falsifies the picture of seventeenth- and eighteenth-century study of language; it violates the most elementary canons of ethics and objectivity. To be blunt, it is a disgrace to scholarship.

5. CONCLUSION. The term LINGUISTICS has been used, in recent times, in at least three senses: (1) speculation about language in general; (2) the technique of grammatical description; (3) an approach to the study of language which is, at least in intent, scientific.[78] In the light of this distinction, the Port-Royal *Grammaire générale et raisonnée* and seventeenth- and eighteenth-century "philosophical grammar" are worthy objects of study from the viewpoint of *linguistics*$_{1,2}$, not of *linguistics*$_3$.[79] The position of the Messieurs de Port-Royal in the history of *linguistics*$_{1,2}$ is secure, as the continuators of an old-established tradition of speculation and grammar, and the initiators of a trend towards increasingly abstract and rationalistic ratiocination.[80] They were intelligent men, and made a worthy contribution. But to modern linguistics (in our third sense), they have virtually no relevance. In fact, as I have pointed out elsewhere,[81] the "general grammar" movement represented a step backward in contrast to the achievements of Italian sixteenth-century scholars (and, for that matter, to some of Ménage's work). We now have an excellent reprint edition of Port-Royal with Brekle's commentary, and a definitive discussion in Donzé's book. From now on, the task of historians of linguistics will be to integrate Brekle's and Donzé's findings into the over-all history of speculation on language and of grammatical formulation.

NOTES

1. Cf. the list given in Brekle (ed.) (1966:xix-xxi).
2. Cf. such discussions as those of Brunot (1913:4.57-60); Harnois (1928:21); Sahlin (1928, passim); Donzé (1967, passim); Kukenheim (1966:41-46); etc.
3. Cf. the detailed discussion of Du Marsais in Sahlin (1928).
4. For Girault-Duvivier, cf. Levitt (1968).
5. For the pendulum-like swings between mentalist and objectivist approaches in linguistics, cf. Esper (1968).
6. Cf. such observations as those of Brunot (1913:4.54);

Sahlin (1928:15-16); Bloomfield (1933a:6-7); Cognet (1950:109-110).
7.   Quotations from Vaugelas are from Chassang (ed.) (1880).
8.   Cf. Cognet (1950).
9.   As all the works of the Port-Royal group were published an-
onymously and authors were referred to collectively as "les Messieurs de Port-Royal", this term is often applied to Arnauld and
Lancelot in connection with their *Grammaire générale*.
10.   Cf. Vaugelas' definition of "le bon usage": "C'est la façon
de parler de la plus saine partie de la cour, conformément à la façon d'escrire de la plus saine partie des autheurs du temps" (Pré-
face, II.3).
11.   For Panzini, see Hall (1951).
12.   Ever since Sainte-Beuve (1954 [1840]:2.479); cf. also Brunot (1913:4;57), Sahlin (1928:14-17, 21, 29, 34-37, etc.); Cognet
(1950:119-110); Kukenheim (1966:30-31); and of course the works
discussed below.
13.   Cf. Donzé (1966:43-44).
14.   Inasmuch as it dealt, in actuality, with primarily two languages, at two specific points of time: Latin of the classical period, and French of their own epoch.
15.   Cf. Brunot (1913:4.3).
16.   Cf. Brunot (1913:4.3-5); Zehnder (1939).
17.   Cf. Hall (1942:46-47).
18.   Cf. Turgot's remarks (Piron [ed.] 1961:5) and Hall
(1964/65).
19.   He was well enough known for Molière to have satirized him
in the personage of Vadius in the *Femmes savantes*.
20.   Cf. Tagliavini (1963:37-40). Tagliavini cites (38) Grö-
ber's observation that 72% of Ménage's first three hundred etymologies agree with those of Diez — showing that the defects in Ménage's method were largely redeemed by his intuitions, and gave results no worse than those of certain amateurish modern etymological
dictionaries.
21.   Cf. Tagliavini's discussion (1963:39) of this latter etymology, including the Chevalier d'Aceilly's quatrain "*Alfana* vient
d'*equus* sans doute, / Mais il faut avouer aussi / Qu'en venant de
là jusqu'ici / Il a bien changé sur la route".
21.   For instance, no mention is made of him in Robins (1967),
the best recent history of linguistics.
22.   Page-references will be made to the facsimile of the third
edition (1676), given in Brekle (1966).
23.   I adhere to the English terminology, in which (as opposed
to that of the Romance languages and Latin), the class of *substantives* includes *nouns* (Fr. *table*, *fauteuil*, etc.) and *adjectives*
(Fr. *bon*, *capable*, etc.).
24.   A rough count was made of each place where one or more languages were referred to (even without quotation of specific forms)
and the number of times for each language was added together, without regard to over-lap.
25.   "Les langues vulgaires" seem to be primarily the modern Romance literary languages of western Europe (French, Italian, Spanish), sometimes German also; examples from this group are usually

from French alone. "Les langues du Nord" are probably the contin-
ental Germanic languages; of English, no mention is made anywhere.
What specific languages are included in "les langues orientales" is
nowhere made clear.
    27. For the class-meanings of the Indo-European personal pro-
nouns, cf. Benveniste (1946). An impersonal like *tonat*, say, simply means 'thundering is going on; neither you nor I are doing it,
nor is specifically more than one protagonist involved'. No subject is possible for such a verb.
    28. This has been a common-place with commentators on Port-
Royal, ever since Sainte-Beuve, who said a century and a half ago
(1954 [1840]:2.475: "On ignorait trop de langues, trop de familles
entières de langues. On construisait avec une simple formule de
pensée ce qui présente une quantité de formes et de diversités im-
prévues dans la nature. [...] D'un certain mécanisme général tout
rationnel, on est venu à la tradition, à la génération historique,
à la vraie physiologie du langage, tandis que, d'Arnauld jusqu'à
Volney, on avait trop accordé à l'abstraction pure". Donzé (1967:
190-191, note 21) remarks: "Sainte-Beuve, avec sa clairvoyance ha-
bituelle, a très bien compris que l'état des recherches au XVIIe
siècle rendait hasardeuse l'entreprise de la grammaire générale".
Cf. also Miss Sahlin's observations (1928:31-33).
    29. Thus virtually all commentators, from Brunot (1913) to
Donzé (1967).
    30. Cf. Robins (1951:74-90, especially 86-87).
    31. Sahlin (1928:8-16); Donzé (1967:25-27).
    32. Sahlin (1928:16). Donzé (1967:27) tries to answer her
point by saying that Arnauld and Lancelot were not trying to discover the truth, but simply to "donner au lecteur une explication
raisonnée d'un ensemble de règles et de connaissances acquises,
réunies en un corps de doctrines organiquement lié, et dont il ne
s'agit pas de démontrer la justesse". But this is just the point:
their "connaissances" were not satisfactorily "acquises", and they
were wrong in thinking that they needed to do no further investigation or discovery. There is still, in the last third of our century, a great deal of work to be done on even our best-known languages, and we are, even now, far from being in a position to develop
a really well-founded theory of general or universal grammar.
    33. Cf. A. N. Chomsky's and his disciples' scorn for "disco-
very-procedures", beginning with Chomsky (1957a).
    34. Despite the denials of Chomsky (1965/66:287-288), it is
well known that almost all seventeenth- and eighteenth-century, and
many nineteenth-century grammarians forced languages of all types
into the mould of Latin structure. If seeing an "ablative" in every French noun introduced by a preposition other than à or *de* (*Gr.
Gén.* II, ch. 6) is not forcing French into a Latin mould, then nothing ever could be. Cf. most recently Longacre (1967:327, fn. 40).
    35. Cf. Hall (1963).
    36. Cf. Nyrop (1925:5.160-169; Foulet (1930:45-49).
    37. Cf. Schwan-Behrens-Bloch (1932:§§302-306), or any other
historical grammar of French.
    38. As pointed out by Miss Sahlin (1928:300).

39. Cf. the observation, in a different connection (that of
town-planning) of Mumford (1961:393): "Unfortunately, baroque plan-
ners assumed that their order was eternal. They not only regiment-
ed space, but they sought to annihilate time". Compare this with
the ideal of fixity in language which Arnauld and Lancelot of
course shared with their times, and which they expressed in the
Grammaire générale (II, ch. 10, end). After arguing that irregularities in usage should not serve as arguments⋯"pour faire douter
des règles & troubler l'analogie", they conclude "Autrement qui
ne s'arrestera qu'aux bizarreries de l'usage, sans observer cette
maxime, fera qu'une langue demeurera toujours incertaine, & que
n'ayant aucuns principes, elle ne pourra jamais se fixer".
     40. Sahlin (1928:228), with the remark "Les faits dont les
auteurs s'occupent ici sont tellement peu généraux que quelques
dizaines d'années plus tard certains d'entre eux n'appartiennent
même plus à l'usage correct du français. L'important pour nous,
c'est que, malgré leurs observations, les auteurs n'ont pas réussi
à éclaircir la nature de l'article".
     41. Cf. Miss Sahlin's observations (1928:417-420), especially
"Nous voilà donc en plein arbitraire: ces théories sont faites sans
aucun égard aux possibilités de la langue. La part de la logique
en elles est assez grande pour fausser la conception des faits lin-
guistiques, et d'un autre côté, les considérations grammaticales
interviennent assez pour empêcher une vraie intelligence de la va-
leur logique de la construction impersonnelle" (418).
     42. Sahlin (1928:101-104), and Donzé (1967:143-145), especial-
ly "Il y a donc confusion entre le plan de la pensée et celui de
son expression verbale; mais passons" (144).
     43. Cf. Donzé (1967:108-112), especially "Arnauld et Lancelot
ne raisonnent pas ici comme des historiens soucieux de retrouver,
dans quam habeo amatam, la structure originelle de la chose que
j'ai aimée, mais comme des logiciens soucieux d'établir, pour la
commodité de leur démonstration, l'existence d'une construction
passive" (110).
     44. Donzé (1967:220) says of this passage: "L'abus de l'ana-
lyse logique touche ici à la naïveté".
     45. As suggested repeatedly by A. N. Chomsky and his disciples.
     46. Cf. Brunot (1913:4.53-57); Kukenheim (1958:30-31).
     47. Cf. Joos (1964:72), with the highly relevant remark "In
certain languages, notably Latin, a finite verb can assert all by
itself, without a subject either spoken or infallibly reconstruct-
ed by the addressee". This latter is an excellent criterion for
the admissibility of an ellipsis.
     48. Brekle (1964, 1967).
     49. With a reference to Chomsky (1964a:15). Such an expansion
is not possible for all adjectives, and it is therefore inaccurate
to interpret every ADJECTIVE + NOUN phrase as derived by ellipsis
from NOUN + RELATIVE PRONOUN + be + ADJECTIVE; cf. Winter (1965).
Port-Royal's and Chomsky's interpretation is a prime example of
what Miss Sahlin (1928:93) called, à propos of Du Marsais' procedures, "une vraie manie de considérer comme elliptiques toutes les
expressions qui sortent du cadre idéal de la phrase type". The

same criticism could, *a fortiori*, be applied to Lancelot's source for this procedure, Sanctius (cf. Mrs. Lakoff's discussion of the last-mentioned [1969]).

50. Donzé (1967).

51. Cf. our discussion (section 2, above) of the narrowly static, absolutist out-look of the French Baroque as reflected in this theory of Port-Royal.

52. We must remember, of course, the extremely short time-perspective afforded by the then prevalent Biblical chronology of man-kind.

53. Coseriu (1957); Foucault (1966, 1967)ñ Chevalier (1967).

54. Snyders (1965).

55. A lesson which was learned much better in the early 1960's than in the later years of the decade; cf. the difference between the intelligent caution shown in the articles contained in Greenberg (ed.) (1963) and the apriorism and neglect of facts manifested in those in Bach and Harms (eds.) (1968).

56. Mok (1968).

57. Chomsky (1966a).

58. As pointed out, somewhat timidly, by Zimmer (1968).

59. Cf. the observation, in connection with Chomsky (1964b, 1965), of Lamb (1967): "A parade of specious arguments, it [*Aspects*] makes liberal use of the shifting meaning, a device which the author has developed to a high degree of refinement. The essence of this device is the shifting of terms from one meaning to another. Supplemented by the complementary stratagem of moving meanings from one term to another, the device is used in attacks upon real or imaginary opponents in mock battles set up for the occasion".

60. Cf. Chomsky (1959), and Esper's critique thereof (1968:225).

61. Cf. Hockett's discussion (1968:62-64) of Chomsky's "Tarzan thinking" in connection with the term *know*. The same type of behavior could be exemplified for many other terms; it is, of course, a type of verbal acrobatics and unacknowledged position-shifting that is at least as old as Plato. Cf. also our note 59.

62. Hall (1964:282; 1968a:21-22).

63. Herdan (1967:35-36), in one of his rather petulant, but thoroughly justified criticism of Chomskyan dogmas. Cf. also Herdan (1968).

64. Cf. Hockett's observation (1968:79-80), especially "The alternative to his [Chomsky's] rationalist views is not eighteenth-century 'scientific naturalism', but twentieth-century empirical science" (80).

65. Cf. Hall (1968a:123-124) and fn. 4 in Hall (1968/69).

66. In addition to our folkloristic belief that whatever is "deep" must be of greater value, etc., than what is "superficial", there is an at least covert appeal to currently wide-spread attachment to Freudian and Jungian theories of "depth-psychology", which — no matter what their absolute validity — have no place in the study of language.

67. What is usually referred to as a "deep structure" is simp-

ly one of a number of possible paraphrases of a construction, selected for the conveenience of deriving the construction from it by
a series of "paper-and-pencil" manipulations (as Esper [1968:222]
calls them). Beyond this, "deep" or "deeper" structure is simply
meaning itself. Now meaning is, as many observers have pointed
out, the correlation existing inside the head of each individual
speaker between linguistic forms or combinations thereof on the one
hand, and the referents of these forms or combinations in the outside world on the other hand (cf. Hall [1968a:22, 62-67]). There
is at present no way of getting at these correlations except by
observing them in speakers' behavior, nor will there be until (as
it now seems) we have some technique for direct examination of what
goes on in and between the various parts of people's brains. Until
then, meaning is — well, not wholly unamenable, but much less amenable to scientific observation than other aspects of language. In
any case, to hypostatize "les mouvemens de l'esprit", "deep structure", or anything of the sort, and then to reify it and treat it
as an objective constant in one's theorizing, is a most elementary
violation of all scientific and philosophical method.

68. Cf. the extensive discussion of recent developments and
the reasons therefor in Hall (1969b).

69. Cf. the observations of Putnam (1967). The further discussion by Chomsky (1968) adds nothing to the elucidation of the
matter.

70. Cf. Hockett (1968:79-81).

71. Cf. Hall (1968a:50-52).

72. Of course, in a democratic society each individual has a
right to his opinion, provided it be expressed within the limits of
courtesy and decency, and not imposed on others by any but majority
rule, but the expression of such opinions should be made "wearing
the hat" of the citizen, not of the scientist., This is an elementary principle, without which both scientific objectivity and freedom of research and report immediately go by the board.

73. E.g. in Chomsky (1967a).

74. Cf. Thomas (1957).

75. Cf., with specific reference to the modern-language-field,
Hook (1969). (And cf. now, with specific reference to Chomskyan
doctrines, Sampson [1979] — RAHjr., 1985.)

76. E.g. Benoit (forthcoming); Predovich (forthcoming). [To
the best of my knowledge, these two items never appeared; but a
rather trenchant criticism was embodied in Hans Aarsleff's two
articles (1970, 1971). — RAHjr., 1985.]

77. E.g. Szépe (1967); Zimmer (1968, albeit with some mild
protests); Prideaux (1968).

78. The classical reference in this connection is Sapir
(1929).

79. The slurs which Chomsky (1966a:101) casts on Leonard
Bloomfield's scholarship, in connection with the picture of the
history of linguistics given by the latter (1933a: ch. 1), are
quite unjustified, since Bloomfield was treating only of linguistics in our third sense. This does not keep one from wishing that
Bloomfield had paid more attention to earlier manifestations, such

as the advances in method made in the Italian Renaissance; but,
on the whole, Bloomfield's picture of the prescientific period is,
with respect to scientific method, still valid.

   70. As Hook points out in another connection (1969:472), one
can hardly blame the initiators of any movement for the excesses
of later comers.

   71. Hall (1942:47-48).

REVIEW OF SALTARELLI, *A PHONOLOGY OF ITALIAN*

(Italica 49.267-272 [1972])

MARIO SALTARELLI: A phonology of Italian in a generative grammar. The Hague — Paris, Mouton, 1970. Pp. 96. (Janua Linguarum, Series Practica, no. 95.)

In the last hundred years, the study of the sounds of language has gone through three major stages. From the 1880's to the 1880's to the 1920's, the phonetician's prime concern was with the analysis and description of speech-sounds themselves. The best frame-work for such description is articulatory, i.e. in terms of the parts of the respiratory system (the "organs of speech") used in sound-production. The classic works representing this approach to Italian are Panconcelli-Calzia (1911) and Camilli (1965).

In the 1930's, 40's and 50's, the phonetic approach was supplemented by greater attention to contrasts between sounds, establishing significant units of sound or PHONEMES, as they function in the structure of language in communication. Linguists of the Prague school (led by N. S. Trubetzkoĭ), the Copenhagen school (inspired by L. Hjelmslev), and a more loosely-knit group of American scholars (following the lead of E. Sapir and L. Bloomfield) took somewhat different approaches to problems of phonemics (or, as it is widely termed in Europe, phonology). Most of them, however, aimed at making phonemics what A. Martinet has termed "functional phonetics". The approaches of these three groups are reflected in Porru (1939), Malmberg (1942/43), and Hall (1948a), respectively.

In addition to the phonemic level, structuralists have recognized another level intermediate between the phonemic and the morphemic, that of morphophonemics, on which phonemes alternate with each other in the variants of a morpheme (a significant unit of linguistic form). Thus, in the Italian forms /díko/ *dico* 'I say' and /díči/ *dici* 'thou sayest', /díče/ *dice* 'he says', /k/ before /o/ alternates with /č/ before /e i/. This alternation can be represented by a morphophonemic symbol, e.g. /K/ , and the root of the Italian morpheme meaning 'say' can be given the single symbolization /diK-/ (as done, say, in Hall [1948a, 1971a]). Many features of conventional orthography are morphophonemic rather than phonemic in their representation of phonological structure: in this case, Italian *c* = /K/.

Since the early 1960's, A. N. Chomsky, M. Halle, and their followers have opposed to structuralism an approach which they claim enables the generation (in the mathematical sense) of linguistic phenomena from an underlying or "deep" structure through a series of transformations, i.e. through the application of various formulae to other formulae, according to specific rules. Description of language in these terms is therefore called TRANSFORMATIONAL-GENERATIVE GRAMMAR (TGG). In phonology, it substitutes rules for functional units, and hence it denies the existence of the phonemic level as such, and the validity of a phonemic transcription. For a phonemic transcription, TGG would substitute one in terms of "underlying representation," as if each morpheme existed independently of sound and were "represented" by a single basic morphophonemic form, from which its phonetic shapes were to be derived by the manipulation of a congeries of rules. To the phonemicist's aim of setting up a biunique transcription, in which one could go unambiguously from sound to phoneme or from phoneme to sound, TGG has opposed an approach in which biuniqueness is not requisite: the only direction considered necessary is that of abstract symbol to sound.

The "underlying representation" is symbolized by alphabetical shapes, but these are considered to represent groupings of "distinctive features". These latter, in Chomsky and Halle (1968) — which has been the principal model for TGG phonological descriptions — are partly articulatory (e.g. tense vs. lax, voiced vs. unvoiced) and partly acoustic-impressionistic (e.g. grave vs. acute). Terms of the latter type, introduced by the Prague school, have been maintained despite the impossibility of defining them objectively (cf. Hall [1950c]). Both articulatory and phonetic features are described, in TGG, in terms of binary choice, indicating their presence or absence (e.g. grave vs. non-grave). For an exposition of the theory of TGG-type phonology as applied to Italian, cf. di Pietro (1970a).

Unfortunately, the TGG approach runs counter to both scientific method and the facts of language (cf. Hall [1969b]). Scientific method involves starting from observed phenomena and proceeding to discover and state (using hypothesis, extrapolation, and proof as necessary) the principles underlying them. TGG, on the other hand, is aprioristic, starting from predetermined notions and forcing the facts into them, or neglecting the facts if they are inconveniently contradictory. Elegance of rules and their "generality" (i.e. applicability to the widest sector of a structure, or the greatest number of languages, possible) is given priority over accuracy. Hence TGG all too often becomes a process of rule-juggling for its own sake. No discussion of language in terms of rules can be of any value, unless the rules are based upon and can be converted into statements of actual fact (cf. Hall [1971, 1972a]).

"Deep structure" in syntax and morphology, and "underlying representation" in phonology, simply do not exist (cf. Hall [1968a]). They are, at best, only *ad hoc* formulations, sources from which the grammarian can, by pencil-and-paper manipulations, derive existing phenomena. The abandonment of the requirement of biuniqueness for phonological formulation slants the description entirely to one

side, that of the speaker. In the actual use of language, speaker
and hearer are of equal importance: the hearer has to decode and
interpret what comes into his ears, and therefore has to go from
the sounds he perceives to their functional units (whatever shape
they may have in his brain, which is something no-one knows as
yet). This is why a phonological formulation must be biunique:
the speaker may possibly be regarded as "deriving" his speech from
a pre-existing internalized morphophonemic system, but the hearer
or reader has to be able to go the other way, from the sound to the
system. (For the importance of taking the listener's point of view
into account in describing linguistic phenomena, cf. Hockett [1961]).
   The book under review, Saltarelli's Illinois Ph.D. disserta-
tion, reflects TGG applied à outrance.   This is evident even in
the organization of the material. Whereas virtually all treatments of phonetics or phonemics describe the sounds of the language and base their discussions of sound-patterning on what has
been presented, S takes all this for granted. After a brief list
of abbreviations (9), he reviews previous "Studies of Italian Pronunciation" (11-20), according to how closely they approximate the
TGG stand-point. His second chapter (21-35) deaks wuth certain
"Problems in Italian Phonology": that of partial complementation,
as posed by [z] and by open è and ò in stressed syllables (21-26);
the relation of stress and length (26-30); the status of (morphophonemic) assimilation (30-31); and the status of constituent
stress (31-35). This chapter contains S's only original contribution to the theory of Italian phonology: the contention that vowel-length, not stress, is significant, and that, on the morphophonemic level, double consonants do not exist. He would therefore
transcribe dote 'dowry' as /dōte/, and -dotte (e.g. in condotte,
dedotte, etc., f.pl.) as ['dot:e] (29-30). Such a transcription
might work for North Italian pronunciation, in which there are no
long consonants and vowel-length is indeed significant; but it cannot apply to standard Italian.

   Why not? Because it clashes with observable facts. S is wrong
in saying it is "generally agreed that the features of stress and
vowel length are concomitant" (29). On the contrary, as I have
pointed out elsewhere (Hall [1971b]), they are not wholly concomitant. Vowel-length can be described wholly as a function of
stress, whereas the converse is not true. Such words as Tàranto,
Òtranto, astracàn 'over-coat', bazàr 'bazaar', màndorla 'almond',
or pòlizza '(insurance-) policy' require their stress to be indicated as such. The last, especially, contradict S's principles, according to which the word for 'almond' ought to be mandòrla, and
that for 'policy' polìzza — but they just aren't. Nor do S's
principles take care of names like Beccarìa, or common words like
baccalà 'cod' or baccarà 'baccarat', in which there are non-morpho-
phonemically determined long consonants before the stress.

   How does one take care of exceptions like these? This is part
of S's concern in the major part of the book, the third chapter,
"A Phonology of Italian" (36-92). It is concerned chiefly with

setting up sequences of rules for deriving Italian phonemes from
aprioristically established "underlying representations". These
are often quite fanciful, e.g. /čiv+tad+e/ for 'city' (5) or
/dok+t+e/ for 'learned' (29-30) (*città* and *dotte*, respectively,
in standard orthography). The first of these can be justified only
by considering words like *civico, civismo, civile* as being, des-
criptively speaking, from the same root· as *città* (which is very
doubtful); the second, by identifying /k/ with the morphophonemic
alternation /K/ discussed above (equally doubtful). The chapter
has five subsections: "3.1. The Phonological System" (36-45);
"3.2. Phonological Redundancy" (45-63); "3.3. Precyclic Rules"
(63-78); "3.4. Phonological Cycle" (78-89); and "3.5. Postcyclic
Rules" (89-92). The bibliography (93-96) is long on listings of
theoretical discussions of TGG, and short on material dealing with
the sounds of Italian.

One of the cardinal tenets of TGG is that syntax is to be described first, then morphology as something determined primarily by
syntax, and lastly phonology, as simply the "realization" o sequences of morphemes. It is therefore considered legitimate to state
in advance of one's phonology whatever exceptions can be formulated
in syntactic or morphological terms. This is what S does in his
§ 3.5, where he discusses features of inflection and derivation to
be taken into account in advance of the phonological description.
He distinguishes between "native" and "non-native" words, so as to
take care of words like *astracàn, baccalà, bazàr, oblò* 'port-hole',
or *bebè* 'baby'. But this assumes that, inside the head of the na-
ive native speaker, there is something which tells him that, say,
città is native and *oblò* is not. In fact, native speakers get very
confused on such points. One such person told me, for instance,
that *ragù* 'ragoût' is a native word because it ends in a vowel!

Likewise, to fit all Italian forms into S's pattern, one must
take care of sequences like *andàtevene!* 'go away!' or *tèmperamela!*
'sharpen it for me!' (sc. *la matita* 'the pencil'). This can be
done by having one's phrasal combinations described in advance of
one's phonology. In this kind of approach, one needs "correct
word-order" (32) established beforehand. But this works, at best,
only for the speaker. The listener knows nothing in advance about
the syntactic or morphological structure of what he has not yet
heard. He has to depend on signals inherent in the sounds he hears.
If, in what is spelled *lavati*, he hears a weak stress followed by a
strong stress, he knows it is to be taken as *lavàti* 'washed (past
part, m.sg.)'' but if he hears a strong stress on the first syllable, followed by weak stress on all the rest, he knows it is *làvati*
'wash yourself! (2nd sg. imper.)'. To get rid of difficulties like
these by treating them in advance of one's main phonological formulation is no solution at all to whatever problems they may pose.
It is merely kicking one's difficulties upstairs.

Aside from his theory of stress and its relation to long consonants, S's description contributes nothing new to our knowledge of

Italian phonology. It is only a restatement of what is already known, in the pseudo-mathematical frame-work of TGG, and with S's erroneous analysis of phonemics and "underlying representation". Decision-tree-diagrams of "distinctive features" (41) or matrices with plus- and minus-signs (92) tell us considerably less about the nature and function of the phonemes, and the respects in which they contrast with each other, than do tables of sounds such as are given in standard works on phonetics. In terms of his own frame-work, S does not go as far as he ought to in analysing the phonemes into their component elements. He still treats /tˢ dᶻ č ǧ/ as separate phonemes, whereas in his system they might just as well be /ts ds tš dš/, respectively, with the appropriate little rules for converting these symbolizations into sounds.

An instructive contrast is furnished by two other recent works on Italian phonology. Muljačić (1969a) is strongly linked to the Prague-school tradition, but gives a solid, thorough discussion, within that frame-work, of Italian phonological structure and contrasts. Lichem (1969) is primarily a work on phonetics, rather than phonemics, intended for German learners of Italian. Muljačić (1969b) has criticized L for insufficient attention to the theoretical aspect of phonemics. Nevertheless (as recognized by di Pietro [1970b]), L's book is also solid and thorough. From either M or L, the reader can get a clear account of the facts of Italian pronunciation and its structure. L's bibliography is much fuller than S's, especially on Italian phonetics. S's view-point, however, is (54): "These rules and their ordering are part of an abstract model attempting to capture a formalization, not of the language user himself but rather of the competence he exhibits in language behavior". But abstract models are worthless unless they are translatable into factual information. As we have seen, S's model fails in this respect, giving an inaccurate representation of the facts of Italian.

Hockett (1968:3-4) has referred to TGG generative phonology as "bankrupt". Chomsky and Halle (1968) and the book under review furnish the best possible evidence for the validity of Hockett's characterization.

"UNDERLYING REPRESENTATION" AND
OBSERVABLE FACT IN PHONOLOGY

(Journal of English Linguistics 7.21-42 [1973])

The distinction between "surface" and "deep" structure, introduced by A. N. Chomsky (1965, and a host of later publications),[1]
has in recent years been extended from syntax to phonology, and has
been rendered especially well known by Chomsky and Halle (1968),
with the term "underlying representation" corresponding to "deep
structure" in syntax. It is my purpose here to show the unfounded
nature of this distinction and the harm that it has done in studies
of phonology.[2] I shall discuss it from three points of view: the
theoretical basis on which it has been established, its application
to the phonology of English, and (more briefly) further extensions
that have been made in applying it to the phonologies of French, I-
talian, and Spanish.

1. THEORETICAL CONSIDERATIONS. In the preface (vii-ix) to
their 1968 book, Chomsky and Halle make a number of statements re-
vealing their basic orientation. Their most important and fundamental assertion is that "a grammar is a theory of a language" (ix).
No statement could be more inexact or farther from the truth. A
grammar can, in and by itself, never be a THEORY of a language; it
can only be a DESCRIPTION of what a language is, i.e. of what its
speakers actually have done when they have spoken and what the pro-
babilities are that they will do when they speak again. (For this
reason, no linguistic analysis or description can ever be anything
but probabilistic.[3]) Any theory concerning a language, or concerning language in general, must emerge from consideration of all a-
vailable data, and is always subject to revision in the light of
new data, no matter how apparently trivial. Otherwise, the theory
ceases to be scientific and becomes a theological dogma.[4]

From this point of view, the Chomskyan-Hallen approach is purely theological, as shown by such statements as "Counterexamples to
a grammatical rule are of interest only if they lead to the construction of a new grammar of even greater generality or if they
show some underlying principle is fallacious or misformulated. Otherwise, citation of counterexamples is beside the point" (ix), or
"a system of transcription or terminology, a list of examples, or a
rearrangement of the data in a corpus is not 'refutable' by evidence apart from inadvertence — errors that are on the level of
proofreading mistakes' (ix). But if primary d ata are not contro-
verible by evidence — or if their controversion is "beside the
point", "trivial", etc.[5] — then, *a fortiori*, no theory based
thereon is so controvertible. (Or, if a theory is not based on
primary data to begin with, it has never been anything but a theo-

logical dogma.) Declaring in advance that one's material is incontrovertible except in a trivial way is a fine method of eluding criticism — and also of removing one's discussion from the realm of scientific inquiry. In fact, as we shall see, many of their statements, of both fact and theory, are highly controvertible, and render their findings well-nigh valueless from any scientific point of view. As has often been observed,[6] errors in basic fact are even more serious than errors in theory.

Another theological aspect of Chomsky and Halle's approach is their apriorism and dualism. Here, as in many others of Chomsky's discussions of language, they start from the (undemonstrated and undemonstrable) assumption that there is a fundamental distinction between a speaker-hearer's competence and his performance, the latter being "based not only on his knowledge of the language, but on many other factors as well — factors such as memory restrictions, inattention, distraction, nonlinguistic knowledge and beliefs, and so forth. We may, if we like, think of the study of competence as the study of the potential preference of an idealized speaker-hearer who is unaffected by such grammatically irrelevant factors" (3). However, as Faust (1970:46) has neatly phrased it, "in effect, Chomsky's ideal speaker-listener is not in a speech-community at all. He is a lone individual, completely surrounded by perfect speech-mirrors." An idealization of an eternally isolated, invariant, perfectly consistent and coherent speaker-hearer's competence is so far removed from any reality as to be an utter impossibility. True, scientists often construct hypothetical models of processes with one or another factor (e.g. friction, momentum) intentionally omitted; but a model such as Chomsky's, with all real-life variables excluded a priori, is valueless for any scientific analysis. In human use of language, all the factors which Chomskyan-Hallean theory systematically excludes — whether they involve relatively consistent and socially conditioned dialectal differences, unpredictable individual nonce-variations, or fluctuations in the frequency of competing alternants — are part of the essence of linguistic structure, not only in performance, but in competence.

As has already been pointed out,[7] the Chomskyan approach continues the mistaken Saussurean notion that linguistic structure is, at any point of time, rigid and invariable. De Saussure also envisaged the language of any community as constituting an "état de langue", self-consistent and logical. This view implies further that some utterances are admissible and others are not, i.e. that there is a distinction between grammatical and ungrammatical, well- and ill-formed sentences. Such a distinction is at the base of Chomsky's theory of language, which, indeed, could not possibly subsist without it. Grammaticality and "well-formedness" are at the base of Chomskyan-Hallean phonology, as well. Thus, they state flatly that "A grammar represents a particular speaker's competence in some language. Since only well-formed grammars are required and since such grammars are acquired in a reasonably short time, the question of well-formedness must be decidable by a procedure that terminates quite rapidly". The latter part of the second sentence just quoted concerns merely the acceptability or otherwise of a particular formal condition for a grammar to be "well-formed"; but the first part of the sentence makes a statement which is diametrically contrary to observed fact. No speaker, in any community, ever has a "well-formed" grammar or system of language-habits; every speaker always has gaps and inconsistencies in his COMPETENCE, not only in contrast to other speakers' usage, but within his own system.[8] "Well-formedness" and "grammaticality" are simply inexistent phantoms, the ghosts of the ancient notions of "correctness" which have been conjured up to lend support to Chomskyan apriorism in dealing with language.

Closely allied to the notion of grammaticality is the procedure of analysing and describing language in terms of rules, instead of statements concerning what speakers actually do. As I have pointed out elsewhere,[9] the notion of RULE — which is very ancient in our inherited procedures of grammatical formulation — can have one of two functions. It can have that of describing phenomena, but in the imperative rather than the declarative ("If you are a man and want to behave as men do in Europe, take off your hat on meeting another man", instead of "Men take off their hats to each other in Europe."); or it can be an order, with greater or lesser sanctions (legal or otherwise), to perform some act ("Keep to the right", "No passing", etc.). The first function involves a mere replacement of one grammatical mood by another; the second is nomothetic, implying the existence of some authority empowered by law or custom to give orders. But there is no room for anything nomothetic in linguistics, by the very nature of the discipline itself.[10] Linguistic norms can be only arbitrary or statistical.[11] In the first case, they have no validity aside from that conferred to them by some outside, non-linguistic power (e.g. the dicta of an academy, supported by governmental force and the prestige of high-ranking social or educational groups). In the second, they of course vary according to actual usage, and are never absolute or permanent. In neither instance can "rules" be set up that "govern" human behavior in any realistic sense.

In any case, language is never "rule-governed", as Chomskyan theory maintains it is. The patterns of linguistic performance and competence are more comparable to path-ways, which people normally follow in their use of language, but not always.[12] On occasion — far more frequently than we usually recognize — every one of us strays from the customary path into some other, usually "adjacent" one. If this happens often enough, a new pattern develops and the lay-out of the path-ways is changed. But humans do not speak according to rule, and there are, at any given time, features of the language of any individual or social group which are not formulatable in terms of rules.[13] The application, in human language, of a theory whose very essence consists of the formulation of rules, can never be anything but harmful, since it restricts its view of human behavior (in language or any other activity) to only those aspects which can be thus formulated, and hence leaves out much that is essential to human communication. No discussion of human behavior in language or any other activity in terms of rules is of any value unless the rules can immediately be reformulated as statements concerning the actual facts — in which case it is better to make the statements of fact to begin with.

But, we have been told repeatedly, rules (and often quite complicated ones, at that) are necessary to transform the "deep structure" into the "surface structure". This brings us to the heart of the matter. Just what is this deep structure? Where does it exist, and what is the difference between it and surface structure? There has been a great deal of discussion of this matter ever since it became a central issue in Chomsky (1965) and following works of his. Even those who accept the notion of "deep structure" are not in agreement as to its nature, particularly as to whether it is grammatical or semantic. From the welter of discussion,[14] there emerges the conclusion that, whether it is the one or the other, it is not accessible to direct observation; that it can be formulated only on the basis of abstractions made from actual speech; and that it is a construct made by the linguist, not anything which a naïve speaker is either aware of or able to formulate.

Skeptics like myself are more inclined to consider the distinction between the two levels of "deep" and "surface" structure as unfounded. These two terms involve a covert appeal to culturally conditioned value-judgements, since in our culture what is "deep" is considered more important than what is on the surface. There is also a parallelism with the (equally questionable) notion of "depth-psychology" in Freudian and Jungian psycho-analysis. In language, we have simply structure — the order, nature, and privileges of occurrence of the linguistic forms which humans use in talking to each other — and meaning. The latter is the associative tie between linguistic sounds and forms on the one hand, and phenomena of the real-life world on the other. It exists inside each individual (particularly, it would seem at present, in his brain), and is neither as highly structured nor as accessible to direct observation as is linguistic form.[15] Most of what, in Chomskyan analyses, is termed "deep structure" is the meaning of a linguistic form or combination of forms. Its formulation in transformational-generative terms is an awkward and needlessly complicated restatement of meaning in pseudo-grammatical guise.[16]

In phonology, Chomsky and Halle have sought to establish a parallel for syntactic "deep structure" in what they term "underlying representation". This concept is based on the assumption that morphemes exist in the abstract in the speakers' minds, and do not "consist" of sounds but are "represented" by them.[17] Each morpheme is is, further, assumed aprioristically to be unitary, and therefore of necessity represented in the abstract by a single sequence of sound-units. In normal language, of course, this is far from being the case, since we all know and recognize such variations as those of the vowel-phonemes in /véyn/ *vain* ~ /vǽnitiy/ *vanity*,[18] /diváyn/ *divine* ~ /divínitiy/ *divinity*, etc., or those of the con- sonant-phonemes in /náyf/ *knife* ~ /náyvz/ *knives*, etc. It has long been the practice to recognize such alternations of phonemes within morphemes, to give their study the special name of MORPHOPHONE- MICS, and to present them by special symbols such as //F // = /f/ ~ /v/.[19]   The Chomskyan-Hallean approach goes well beyond already recognized morphophonemics, however, by insisting that the "repre- sentation" underlying all such alternations (in derivation and in syntactically determined sandhi, even more than in inflection) is universally present in linguistic structure, is more fundamental than what has by most linguists been termed phonemics, and is not only a construct set up by the analyst of language, but a psycho- logical reality as well.[20]

This view of phonological structure is implemented, in Chomsky- an-Hallean theory, by an adaptation of the "distinctive feature" approach developed by Román Jakobson.[21] The insufficiences of this approach, especially in its use of vague, impressionistic pseudo-a- coustic terms such as "acute," "grave," "compact," "diffuse," and its dependence on undemonstrated factors such as "saturation", have repeatedly been pointed out.[22]   Chomsky and Halle dilute this Ja- kobsonian impressionism by introducing a certain number of features which are derived, not from acoustic, but from articulatory phone- tics, such as nasality, tenseness, and laxness. Clearly, the over- simplified Jakobsonian frame-work was simply inadequate to handle the facts of English, and had to be expanded somehow. The result, however, is an incoherent mixture of pre-Jakobsonian and Jakobson- ian analyses, which is really satisfactory from neither point of view.

For their theoretical basis, therefore, Chomsky and Halle use an aprioristic, theological set of concepts, which produce an im- aginary speech-situation with an idealized speaker-hearer who could never exist anywhere, using a rigid system with an impossibly "well-defined" or "grammatical" set of rules. They hypothesize an undemonstrable "deep structure," which in phonology is really mor- phophonemics, but a morphophonemics which is schematized out of — well, not absolutely all, but almost all resemblance to reality, and which requires a tremendously complicated set of formulae to bring it into any such resemblance. Let us now see what they do in applying this theory to the sounds of English.

2. ENGLISH PHONOLOGY. It is well known that English has two chief lexical strata, the "popular" and the "learnēd".[23] (There are, of course, no sharp boundaries between the two, since some words are intermediate in their characteristics.) The former are characterized mainly by brevity (one or two sullables), simplicity of syllable-structure, and semantic relation to relatively every- day and essential aspects of living. To this group belong not only a great many Germanic words (*hand, foot, man, wind, fire*, etc.) but also a number of early loans from Latin such as *church* and *wine*,

and of mediaeval borrowings from Romance (especially Old French),
e.g. *chair, vest, table, move*, and many others which the ordinary
speaker of present-day English does not know are non-Germanic in
origin.[24] The learnēd stratum, in contrast, contains polysyllabic
words with a more complicated syllable-structure, and relating in
general to a more advanced, abstract level of intellectual activity, e.g. *polysyllabic, syllable, structure, intellectual, activity.*[25] In between these two types fall such words as *resemble, remember, encounter, enter, entrance* — most of them loans from
French, but less completely assimilated into the "popular" English
vocabulary than those cited in the fourth sentence of this paragraph.

The words of Germanic origin are generally recognized to be the
most "basic" of the English vocabulary, by virtue of both their semantic importance and their text-frequency. Chomsky and Halle,
however, base by far the largest part of their discussion and argumentation on the Graeco-Latin elements in English vocabulary. To
substantiate this assertion, Table 1 shows the proportions of words
of Germanic, Graeco-Latin,[26] Romance (particularly French), and o-
ther origin in (a) the items listed on p. 457 in Chomsky and Halle's index of words from *Mississippi* through *pawn*; (b) the words
in the same alphabetical range (*miss* through *pass*) in the list of
the five hundred most frequent words (1-500) as counted by Thorndike and Lorge (1944:268); and (c) the words in the same alphabetical range (*modern* through *pair*) in the next most frequent five
hundred words (501-1000) in Thorndike and Lorge (1944:269). Obviously, as is well known, the proportion of Graeco-Latin and Romance elements goes up, in text-frequency, as we get into the less
frequent words. One would have to go very far indeed to reach, in
text-frequency, the proportion of Graeco-Latin vocabulary on which

TABLE 1

By origin

	Germanic	Graeco-Latin	Romance (mostly French)	Other
Chomsky-Halle	29 (17%)	99 (55%)	36 (21%)	6 (4%)
T-L 1-500	40 (77%)	5 (10%)	7 (13%)	——
T-L 501-1000	15 (38%)	14 (36%)	10 (26%)	——

Chomsky and Halle base the major part of their analysis. Many of
their items are, indeed, highly specialized terms (e.g. *morbil-
lose, ornithofauna, oscilloscope*), which the normal speaker of the
language would hardly know without special training in the appropriate field. One cannot treat the lexicon of a language as if it
were a single monolithic unit, all items of which are equally well
known to all speakers.[27] This is the static approach of the stud-

ent of a dead language or of a dictionary, not that of the linguist
who recognizes the existence of diversity on the idiolectal and
dialectal level and of fluctuation leading to continual though
gradual change.

By basing the main part of their analysis on the morphophonemics of learnèd words, Chomsky and Halle are led into a maze of com-
plications, which they force onto the structure of non-learnèd
words. At the very out-set, in their "first approximation" of the
"segmental phonology of English" (28-29), they introduce a transcription using the symbols i o æ u ʌ ə for the "simple" vocalic nuclei in *pit, pet, pat, pat, put, putt,* and the second syllable of *analyse*; and capital I E A U O for the "complex"
ones of *confide, feel, fade, feud* and *road,* respectively. The
choice of these latter five symbols is obviously dictated by their
use in English conventional spelling, and particularly by the use
of the same letter for different vocalic nuclei in alternation in
such pairs of learnèd words as /néyšən/ *nation* ∿ /nǽšənəl/ *national.* Stress is then declared to be assigned automatically within
the word, according to a distinction between "weak" (W) clusters
and "strong" (S) ones. The former are sequences consisting of a
simple vocalic nucleus plus no more than one consonant, and the
latter contain a vocalic nucleus followed by two or more consonants, or else a complex vocalic nucleus followed by any number of
consonants. (The Bloomfield-Trager-Smith approach would have made
the statement of this principle much easier, but it clearly did not
suit Chomsky and Halle's purposes to recognize "complex" vocalic
nuclei as consisting of VOWEL + SEMI-VOWEL.)

Then we are told that primary stress is automatically assigned
to the final syllable of words like *eváde, suprême, exíst, absúrd*
(all having final "strong" clusters), but to the penultimate syllable of words with final "weak" clusters, e.g. *rélish, cóvet, de-
vélop, stólid, cómmon, clandéstine.* (Notice that these are almost
all learnèd words.) So far, so good, as long as only words of this
type are involved; but what about such derivatives as *pérsonal,
theátrical, anecdótal, dialéctal* (31-33)? These are exceptions,
and have to be taken care of by further modifications of the rules
already set up: in this instance, by providing for a different assignment of stress in case an affix is involved. Each of these and
later modifications is accompanied by extensive theoretical discussion of the way in which rules are to be formulated and interpreted, with much use of quasi-algebraic notation.

From this point on, the rest of the book is devoted to more and
more extsnsive "refinement", i.e. complication, in the rules given
and the notation proposed for the "underlying representation" of
English words. Even where their analysis would seem, at first
glance, to simplify the system which they assume as basic, this effort causes further complexity, particularly in their effort to eliminate two phonemes, /a/ (as in "General American" *hot, cot, logic*) and /ɒ/. To get rid of the latter, they assume that phonetic

word-final or intervocalic [ŋ], as in *sing*, *singer*, is the result
of a fusion of NASAL + /g/ in word-final position or before an affix (85). The trouble with this is that there are exceptions, such
as *dinghy*, *hangar*, *gingham*, *Birmingham* (234; one could add others,
such as the Ohio place-name *Muskingum*). These would seem to require /ŋ/ as an independent phoneme. But no: we must assume that
these forms have such underlying representations as /dinxi/,
/xænxr/, etc. Standard British or American English has no sound
[x], but this does not worry Chomsky and Halle. They assume it for
such a word as *right*, for which they propose the "underlying representation" /rixt/.[28] (Why we should assume /x/, rather than /h/,
as the initial consonant of *hangar*, we are not told.) In any case,
to assume that intervocalic, non-morphologically-related [ŋ] is e-
qual to /nx/ does not simplify matters at all. It only kicks one's
difficulties into another section of the over-all formulation. What
do we gain by reinterpreting a real sound as reflecting a sequence
of another sound plus a non-existent one?

A similar instance of involved and unrealistic manoeuvering, to
get rid of an inconvenient "surface" phenomenon, is found in Chomsky and Halle's assumption of "underlying" final /e/ in such words
as *menu*, *cue*, *value*, *fuel*, which they transcribe as /menue/, /kue/,
/vælue/, /fuel/ (196). This they follow with the statement that
"Phonetic contrasts such as *cow* — *cue*, or *foul* — *fuel* — *mule*
[...] do not require new phonological segments; rather, they result
from the lexical contrasts /ku/ — /kue/, /fūl/ — /fuel/ — /mule/.
Words such as *immune*, *commute*, *inure*, *cutaneous* will be derived
from the underlying forms /imune/, /kɔN-mute/, /inure/, /kutæni +
əs/, respectively" (196). (Why not /iN-mune/, by the way?) This
is all fantastic nonsense. There is no final vowel [e] or [ə] in
any of the words involved, and there is no justification for tack-
ing on a non-existent vowel. Most of these words are monosyllabic,
including also *pule*; but *fuel* is always bisyllabic, and *mule* is monosyllabic for some, but bisyllabic for others.[29] The only reason
The only reason for marking a final /e/ in these words, in the present-day language, is that they are written with *-e* in English orthography. The height of absurdity is reached in postulating
(147-148) a completely imaginary final /e/ in such words as
/bVrleske/, /Elipse/, /sEmente/ (*burlesque*, *ellipse*, *cement* [!]),
merely in order to make these words fit into their dogmas concerning assignment of stress to a final syllable. Straightforward and
direct representation of the actual facts of language is apparently very far down in the scale of Chomskyan-Hallean priorities, as
compared with rendering their paper-and-pencil manipulations smooth
(though by no means simple!).[30]

A third instance of grossly unrealistic representation, ground-
ed solely in orthography, is Chomsky and Halle's ascription of
double consonants to English (148-153). In fact, English has no
double consonants at all in single words, except between morphemes,
either in phrases (e.g. *hot time*) or across open juncture in com-
pounds (e.g. *port-tax*). However, one of Chomsky and Halle's basic

principles seems to be that, if a sound or sequence of sounds does not appear in a language, that is all the more reason for ascribing it to the "underlying representation," often in order to get rid of the necessity of including an inconvenient phoneme that does exist (cf. our discussion of /ŋ/ in the second preceding paragraph). Again, because double consonant letters often serve to indicate the position of stress in English orthography, they ascribe double consonants to their "underlying representation," referring to this procedure, in a rare outburst of candor, as an "artifice" (148). Thus they arrive at representations like /kVress/, /kwiess + ent/, /æckwiesse/ or /æckwiesce/, and /giræffe/, justifiable only because these words are spelled *caress, quiescent, acquiesce,* and *giraffe,* respectively.

In fact, however, these methodological gaffes on the part of Chomsky and Halle serve simply to demonstrate that their basic claim — that stress is automatic in English words — is unjustified. Writing final double consonant-letters and final /e/ where none exist in speech is merely a graphic procedure which takes the place of a much simpler device, the writing of an accent-mark over the vowel-letter of the syllable involved. In other words, they have unwittingly proven the opposite of what they set out to prove: they have shown definitively that stress is phonemic in English. They have also shown that, in order to replace a straightforward and easily comprehensible symbol like an accent-mark indicating phonemic stress, one can construct a whole congeries of rules and take over artifices like unpronounced double consonant letters and final /e/ from orthography, to indicate the same phenomenon, devoting a long book to the task and obfuscating the entire situation in the process.

Chomsky and Halle claim that "with the postulation of double consonants, just as with the postulation of final /e/, we fill a gap in underlying structure (a phonological gap) and extent the symmetry of the system of lexical entries" (150). Filling gaps and smoothing out asymmetries would seem to be, for them, far more important than "telling it like it is." What would we think of a map-maker who changed the data on his map to accord with the Biblical prediction "Every valley shall be exalted, and every mountain and hill shall be made low, and the crooked shall be made straight, and the rough places plain" (Isaiah 40.4)? The task of the linguist is in many ways similar to that of the map-maker, and his final result should be something like the figures on the left in Table 2. Chomsky and Halle's portrayals of linguistic phenomena, on the other hand, are like those on the right. Why should we try to fill in gaps or extend symmetries to places where they do not exist, when the existence of gaps and asymmetries is observed in the structure of language itself, to be gotten rid of only at the expense of denying reality?

These are only a few, and perhaps the most fantastic, of the many misrepresentations at which Chomsky and Halle arrive, by an

TABLE 2

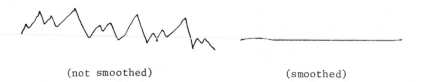

(not smoothed)   (smoothed)

TWO REPRESENTATIONS IN A MOUNTAIN-RANGE IN PROFILE

TWO REPRESENTATIONS OF A PAIR OF RAILWAY-ROUTES
(with stations in towns A, B, and C)

extensive process of rule-formulation and -juggling. They do not let the facts of the language determine what their rules are to be, and how far they can go in establishing them. Rather, they start with an *idée fixe*: that English stress is, at all costs, to be treated as non-phonemic. To this end, they set up a series of rules, exceptions, subsidiary rules to take care of the exceptions, further adjustments to deal with new exceptions that arise as a result of the subsidiary rules, and so on *ad infinitum*. In the end, as we have just observed, they prove the opposite of what they started out to prove. Many of their formulations reflect existing morphophonemic alternations, and would of course be useful in recognizing types of gradation and in establishing "canonical forms", as done by Francis (1958:208-218), Smith (1968), and others. But there is a wide gap between doing this for forms which actually show such alternations, and unjustifiably extending the principle to other forms which do not show them (e.g. *lot, spa,* and a great many others) and then engaging in unbridled (but ultimately futile) formulaic gyrations so as to work the latter in.)

The final formulation at which Chomsky and Halle arrive (236) for their putative vowel-system of English is shown in Table 3. It looks deceptively simple, involving only six simple vowels plus tenseness (which they symbolize with the macron) and also distinctive rounding for the low tense vowels, giving fourteen in all: /i e æ u o ɔ ī ē ǣ ū ō ɔ̆ ǽ/. But in the following pages (237-245), they enumerate no less than forty-three highly complicated rules by the application of which one is to derive the "surface" phenomena from the (often very different) "underlying

TABLE 3

	- back - round	+ back + round
+ high - low	i	u
- high - low	e	o
- high + low	æ	ɔ

LAX VOWELS OF "UNDERLYING REPRESENTATION IN ENGLISH
PHONOLOGY (CHOMSKY AND HALLE, p. 236)

representation". However, this latter, far from being a reasonable abstraction from the phonetic facts of the language, closely resembles the incomplete, incompetent respellings furnished by the editors of third-rate dictionaries as "pronunciation-guides". What is the use of going through such a tremendous process of theorizing and rule-juggling, only to come out with a result so complicated, so out of touch with any present-day reality, and at the same time so old-fashioned and long since deservedly discredited? Part of the answer lies in the fact that, as Hammarström (1971:107) points out, they have let diachronic considerations influence their analysis, but their formulations "taken as diachronic statements [...] are incomplete and unoriginal".

Many of Chomsky and Halle's rules reflect historical developments, e.g. diphthongization, tensing, and vowel-shift (Chapters 4 f.). This, too, is nothing new; it has been known for a long time that morphophonemic alternations often (though not always) reflect historical developments and sound-changes. Here again, however, Chomsky and Halle push their claims far beyond any reasonable position. They devote a whole chapter (no. 6) to what they consider the sound-patterns of English to have been in earlier centuries, as shown in their re-interpretation of the writings of John Hart, John Wallis, Christopher Cooper, and T. Batchelor. Their over-all view of linguistic change (249-259) is highly unrealistic, since it is based on the addition or subtraction of mere rules to the grammar of a language. In reality, rules do not change, nor do they spread;[31] what changes is people's habits of saying things and the meanings of what they say. The vowel-system of English has not (as Chomsky and Halle allege) shown "great stability" (289). On the contrary, it has changed extensively, due to the well-known historical processes of vowel-shift and diphthongization, which Chomsky and Halle's procedures mask almost wholly by incorporating them as mere rules in a pseudo-descriptive analysis.

The customary view of English orthography is that, among modern spelling-systems, it is exceptionally ill-suited for its purpose, the representation of the sound-system of the language. Chomsky and Halle go to the opposite extreme, declaring flatly that "English orthography, despite its often cited inconsistencies, comes remarkably close to being an optimal orthographic system for English" (49), a statement which they repeat later nearly verbatim (184, n. 19). Of course, English orthography is "optimal" for reflecting an alleged "underlying representation" which is, as pointed out above, based almost wholly on English orthography itself. For representing the facts of English phonology, however, our spelling is neither optimal nor pessimal, though by no means as close to optimal as the orthographies of (say) Italian, Hungarian, or Finnish. Even with due allowance for the use of letters (especially vowel-letters) to stand for morphophonemic alternations, there is still enough looseness of fit between sound and letter (think of such unmotivated free variations as those between *pain* and *pane*, *bear* and *bare*, *Gerry* and *Jerry*) to render English spelling definitely non-optimal.

Chomsky and Halle's efforts to read significant stress out of court in English phonology depend also on their assumption that morpho-syntactic criteria are not only admissible, but necessary in determining phonological analysis. Thus, if we know in advance that, say, *contrast* is a noun, it will in general be stressed on the first syllable; if a verb, on the second. There are two basic objections to this assumption. In the first place, the speaker may know in advance that he is going to use a given word as a noun or as a verb; his hearer does not.[33] In many utterances, it is only from the position of the stress that a hearer knows whether, say, *contrast* is to be taken as a noun or as a verb. Secondly, there are a great number of instances in which such words as *permit*, *protest*, etc. are consistently stressed by many speakers in a different way from what "the rules" prescribe (e.g. *permít* as a noun, or *prótest* as a verb). We can always declare these pronunciations to be "ungrammatical" and thus sweep them under the carpet; or one can simply list them as exceptions, though their number and constituency are always changing. But if we do not take these easy ways out, the existence of even one such habitual variation knocks Chomsky and Halle's entire theory of morphologically determined stress into a cocked hat. In both the short and the long run, it is far simpler and more in accord with the facts to recognize / ´/ as a significant element in the phonological structure of every word, than it is to indulge in incredibly long, complicated, and highly unrealistic sequences of rules and artifices without succeeding, after all, in demonstrating its non-existence.[34]

In this large book of 484 pages, purporting to set forth THE sound-pattern of English, Chomsky and Halle have given us a prize example of how far aprioristic theory can go in twisting and misrepresenting the facts of language, merely to come out with an "underlying representation" based on an orthography which is, as we

all know, misleading and in part unmotivated. They have devoted a
large proportion of their book (I have not counted pages and lines)
to extensive discussion of the formulation and ordering of rules —
a topic which may be germane to mathematics or logic, but which has
no relevance to linguistics. With regard to English, they have
succeeded only in proving two things, one of them against their declared intent: (1) that stress is not predictable and is therefore
phonemic, and (2) that present-day morphophonemic alternations reflect phonemic splits that have taken place since Old English times.
We knew both of these things long ago. Horace said (*Ars Poetica*
139) *Parturient montes, et nascitur ridiculus mus*; but in all such
parturitions, few such ridiculous mice as this one can have appeared.

The harmful effect of such pretentious distortion of priorities, procedures, and results is to be seen, not only in much current theorizing concerning the phonology of English, but also in
recent presentations of other languages' sound-systems, three of
which I shall discuss very briefly.

3. FRENCH, ITALIAN, AND SPANISH PHONOLOGY. Recently, the
phonology of French has been treated by Schane (1968), that of
Spanish by J. Harris (1969), and that of Italian by Saltarelli
(1970), according to the principles of generative phonology. All
three of these treatments distort their respective languages at
least as much as Chomsky and Halle do with English, and perhaps, in
the case of French, even more so. This is not the place for an extensive discussion of these treatments,[35] but we may briefly indicate certain characteristics, deriving from the Chomskyan-Hallean
approach, which they all have in common.

Most important, perhaps, is their extensive use of derivational
morphophonemic relationships to motivate their departure from phonetic fact in setting up their "underlying representations." Thus,
Schane uses such transcriptions as |hAlt| for *haut* 'high' and
|fEsta| for *fête* 'feast' (55), and |ʃAnt=ɔr#| for *chanteur* 'sing-
er', |pAtis=ɛr#| for *pâtisseur* 'baker', |dAn=ez+a| for *danoise* 'Da-
nish' (f.sg.), |dɛ=ven+t| for *devient* '(he) becomes' (62), and
many others equally far removed from the actual pronunciation.
Likewise, Saltarelli claims that the "underlying form" of Italian
/čittáˣ/[36] *città* 'city' is /čiv+tād+e/ (5), and that of Italian
/dótte/ *dotte* 'learned (f.pl.)' is /dok+t+e/ (29-30). These iden-
tifications are based on derivational relationships, e.g. French
/festẽ/ *festin* 'banquet' : /fet/ *fete*, or the presence of /or/
in a suffix like /orial/ -*orial* : /œr/ -*eur*,, or Ital. /čiv-/
civ- in such forms as /čívico/ *civico* 'civic'. But the question immediately arises as to how far such derivational relationships
should be considered valid. This is a particularly difficult problem in French, as in English, because of the co-existence of learned, semi-learned, and popular forms. To what extent are we justified in consolidating, say, French /žwaɲ-/ *joign-* 'join', /žwɛ̃t-/
joint- in /ˇzwɛ̃tyr/ *jointure* 'juncture' and the like, and /žõnkt-/

jonct- in /žõksjõ/ *jonction* 'junction' (or, for that matter, their English counterparts) under one single formula? No definitive answer can be given at this time;[37] but the Chomsky-Halleans show no hesitation in going to extremes for both inflectional and derivational relationships, in order to esbalish a single unified base-form.[38] (Not even Schane, however, could devise a formula to cover cases of suppletion like /al-/ *all-* ∿ /v-/ *v-* ∿ /i-/ *i-* 'go' in French, or /gow-/ *go-* ∿ /wen-/ *wen-* in English.[39])

Of course, to replace these symbols by others, or to delete them from the final product, nearly endless sequences of rules and orders of application — forty-five rules in Schane's case (157-58) — are necessary, rendering the process of interpretation of the "underlying forms" highly difficult. Many of these scholars' rules, like those of Chomsky and Halle, are necessitated by the introduction of unjustified historical considerations, e.g. the development of Modern French /'o^/ *haut* 'high' out of Old French /halt/ *halt*; the existence of Latin and Proto-Romance /-t-/ as a past-participle-ending; or that of /-a/ as a feminine singular noun- and adjective-ending. As mentioned above, many a morphophonemic relationship does point back to an earlier situation; but this is no excuse for interpreting the present-day language as continuing, nearly *in toto*, the state of affairs of a thousand or more years ago.

Another feature that these treatments have in common with Chomsky and Halle is their insistence on making the "underlying representation" as different as possible from the picture generally given in earlier descriptions of the phonetics and phonemics of the language involved. Is English and Italian stress normally considered significant? Chomsky-Halle and Saltarelli will knock themselves out (and, in the process, the facts as well) to eliminate it from their systems. Do thousands of French words like /fɛt/ *faite* 'done (f.sg.)' end in a consonant-sound? Such scholars as Trager and Togeby have already suggested that they be regarded as nevertheless ending in /-ə/; Schane will go them one better and assume that this /ə/ represents an "underlying" |a|. Is there a front-rounded series of vowels /y ø œ/ in present-day French? Schane will eliminate it by pushing the entire vowel-scheme back to the situation that prevailed ca. 800 A.D. All observers have considered that Spanish has only five vowel-phonemes; but J. W. Harris, in order to eliminate morphologically related diphthongization from his "underlying representation", introduces non-existent lax vowels (74). If vowel-length is usually considered non-significant, and consonant-length significant, in Italian, Saltarelli will maintain (wrongly, as I have pointed out [Hall (1972c)]) that the opposite is the case. The result of such procedures is only to *épater les bourgeois*, without demonstrating anything really new or true about the language concerned. One is reminded of the limerick about "modernistic" music:

> To compose a sonata today,
> Don't proceed in the old-fashioned way:
>   With your toes on the keys
>   Bang the floor with your knees;
> "Oh, how modern!" the critics will say.

In a few respects, these books, especially Schane's, represent a slight improvement over the methods of Chomsky and Halle (1968). Schane at least uses a special pair of marks │ │ to enclose his "underlying representations," and distinguishes these latter clearly from his straight phonemic transcriptions, which he places between slant lines / / in the customary fashion. This is better than Chomsky and Halle's misleading habit of using the slant lines, not for anything resembling true phonemic transcriptions, but for their own re-interpretations, thereby confusing their readers. Schane rightly recognizes that liaison and elision belong together as aspects of the same morphological phenomenon, although his treatment of them is inadequate.[40]

4. CONCLUDING REMARKS. After discussing his four examples of "nonsense-linguistics", of which Chomsky and Halle (1968) is the last, Hammarström says (1971:108-109):

> Common to all authors quoted is obviously an ambition to write real and original linguistics. They are, however, lacking self-critical capacity. [...]

> Case 4 is the case of two authors who have been carried away by a complex of fashionable ideas, be they or be they not a continuation of older tradition. [...] They are so busy establishing and applying the dogmas of their faith that they do not notice that the description of the "sound pattern" of English becomes absurd.

> Many nonsense studies have been published at the expense of the author. This, however, is not so in any of our four cases. [...]

> In case 4 it is no wonder that the work was published. The first author is considered by a considerable part of now living linguists as a great leader and the other author is also a known linguist.

If one agrees — as I do — with Hammarström's evaluation of Chomsky and Halle (1968), two questions arise: (1) How could the present situation have come to pass? and (2) What can be done to set matters straight?

To the first question, the answer is complicated, and we must, as I have already suggested (Hall [1969b]), recognize at least four factors. The exaggerations of previous approaches, especially the

type of "structuralism" practised by Z. S. Harris and others, had
made the field ready for a pendulum-like swing.[41] Linguistics has
had an influx of persons from other fields, particularly mathematics and logic, in which formulaic manipulations, carried out with
pencil and paper, play a dominant rôle. The "generation-gap" of
the 1960's has persuaded many untrained or only partially trained
younger persons that "whatever is, is wrong", and made them ready
to follow blindly the leadership of any charismatic personality of
whose extra-linguistic (especially political) opinions they may be
enamoured. At the same time, many equally untrained older persons
— especially teachers of English and foreign languages — have
felt insecure because the findings of structural linguistics seemed
to pose a threat to them. Such a situation has rendered linguistics fatally vulnerable to doctrines which were superficially at-
tractive because of their apparent mathematical and logical exacti-
tude; which offered opportunities for unlimited manipulation of
formulae couched wholly in visual symbols, and which called for no
no knowledge of any language beyond one's native tongue, no technical training in first-hand work with other languages, and no discarding of culturally determined folkloristic superstitions concerning language.[42] They have provided an excellent opportunity to
appear ultra-modern and yet to produce nothing beyond restatements
of out-worn dogmas, comparable to the wrinkles of old apples con-
cealed by the deceptive brilliance of sparkling cellophane. Notoriety, under these circumstances, is easily gained, and a reputa-
tion for originality is easily acquired, no matter how little deserved.

What is to be done? Both negative and positive measures are
called for. The serious inadequacies of the Chomskyan-Hallean and
other idealistic-theological approaches must be examined and discussed critically, as some scholars have already begun to do.[43]
At the same time, the material which they have covered must be re-
examined and as much of it as possible salvaged. In this case, the
morphophonemics of English learnēd vocabulary, which was sketched
very briefly by Bloomfield (1933b) and for which Chomsky and Halle
have gathered a considerable amount of material, should be re-ana-
lysed and re-formulated intelligibly and intelligently. Perhaps,
if this is done, Chomsky and Halle (1968) may prove to have been of
some use after all.

NOTES

1. The use of a similar contrast by Hockett (1958, ch. 29), in
speaking of "surface and deep grammar", does not refer to anything
resembling the Chomskyan dualism, but reflects Hockett's particular
view of the relation of linguistic structure to the non-linguistic
universe. I used the expression "relatively surface grammar and
deep-level grammar" (Hall [1966:110-111]), referring to the distinction between inflection and word-formation in morphology. This
use, derived from Hockett's, was unfortunate, and I would no longer
formulate the relationship in these terms.

2. I am, of course, not the first to voice criticisms; cf. the
highly pertinent and cogent observations of Householder (1965, 1966)
and those of Hammarström (1971), whose technique is reminiscent of
that of Bloomfield (1944). Hockett s characterization of the Chomskyan-Hallean orientation as "a strange new slant toward phonology"
(1968:4) and as "completely bankrupt" (1968:3) is certainly valid,
but insufficiently documented at that point.
3. As LePage (1971:430) has felicitously phrased it, "All grammar is an analysis of past events; we apply it to the future at our
peril".
4. I am, on the basis of extensive observation of the use of
the terms THEOLOGY and SCIENCE, defining them as follows:

A theology is a set of statements brooking no contradiction (dogmas), cerning forces or beings (e.g. deities,
spirits, angels, devils, souls) which are not accessible
to human observation in any controllable or verifiable
fashion, but whose existence, permanent importance, and
supreme power is assumed a priori, and is considered an
undeniable, irrefutable factor which has to be taken into
account as determining everything else in the study or
discussion of the universe.

A science is a method for arriving at statements which
brook contradiction, concerning only phenomena which are
accessible to human observation or are deducible on the
basis of observation; whose existence is assumed only on
the basis of hypotheses which can be tested, checked,
and confirmed by procedures accessible to all observers;
and whose function in the study or discussion of the universe is never considered permanently undeniable or irrefutable.

5. Who is defining "beside the point", "trivial", "uninteresting", and similar terms which recur constantly in all Chomskyan
discussions? Here, too, the use of such terms is simply a device
to fend off in advance all inconvenient interference from objections based on such nugatory considerations as those raised by
mere data, mere observable facts.

6. Cf. the saying (ascribed to Niels Bohr, though I have been
unable to check the reference) that there are two kinds of errors,
those due to insufficient theoretical foundation and those due to
inaccurate data — and that, of the two kinds, the latter are the
more serious.
7. E.g. by Hockett (1968:11-13, 57) .
8. I have emphasized this elsewhere (Hall 1968a:20, 87-91).
More recently, Householder (1972) and Anttila (1972: ch. 3) have
rightly based their views of the nature of linguistic change on
the necessarily incomplete character of individual and social linguistic systems, with resultant competition between variants for
acceptance by one group or another.

9. Hall (1972a).

10. As I have repeatedly emphasized ever since the publication of Hall (1950a).

11. Cf. Hall (1975a).

12. Where the order of elements is fairly well fixed, as in English, French, and most other modern Indo-European languages, these path-ways can be represented two-dimensionally, in diagrams showing the sequences which occur and a speaker's choice among them, once he has embarked on any given construction. I have tried to do this at some length in Hall (1969a) (which might better have been entitled *Pathways Through Sentences*) and (1971a).

13. Cf. Behre (1967), and the remarks of Strang (1969), especially "Since the findings show distribution to be other than random, there are constraints to be discovered and stated; the statement of them in almost every case shows that a rule-formulated grammar could not handle the evidence" (234).

14. A few items out of many, chosen simply to exemplify the diversity of opinions: Winter (1965), Evers (1968), Brekle (1969), Coseriu (1969), McCawley (1969), Chafe (1970).

15. This is, of course, the reason why it has normally been considered more profitable to begin linguistic analysis from the angle of form than from that of meaning (cf. my discussion in Hall [1972b]).

16. Thus, for instance, the long series of partly imaginary steps set forth by Langacker (1968:59) for "deriving" the French noun-construction with possessive adjective from a "deep structure" of the verb *être* 'to be' + *à* 'to' + PRONOUN: e.g. *mon livre* 'my book' ← *le livre est à moi* 'the book is to me = is mine'. This is simply a needlessly complicated way of saying what we all knew already, namely that the French possessive adjective is a determiner in the noun-phrase and combines in itself the meaning of the definite article with pronominal reference to a possessor.

17. This dualistic approach has distant antecedents in the comparison — frequent ever since antiquity — of thought as something on a loftier level which is "realized" and brought down, as it were, into speech. Typical of this infelicitous metaphor is the remark of Claudio Tolomei (in his dialogue Il Cesano, ca. 1535) concerning one of the interlocutors: sciogliendo quel nodo a' pensieri che li sosteneva, così nella lingua scender li fece 'Untying that knot in his thoughts which held them up, he brought them down (lit. made them descend) into language in this way' (quoted in Hall (1936:98).

18. Although it is not perfect, the transcription of English set forth in Trager and Smith (1951) is used here for typographical convenience. Those who prefer a notation closer to that of the IPA (as modified by Kenyon [1924]) can easily make an almost wholly automatic reformulation for themselves.

19. Cf. the discussion in Hockett (1958: ch. 33); Gleason (1962:83, 116, 389); Hall (1964: ch. 23).

20. To uphold this last point, supporters of the Chomskyan-Hallean view-point are in the habit of citing Sapir (1933), disregarding the wholly different point of his argument, which was that

phonemes are units of structure which correspond to something existing inside each speaker's head as well as in his manifest beha-
vior-patterns — a point which even the most convinced behaviorist
would be perfectly willing to admit. Sapir's concept of the phoneme (as shown, say, in Sapir [1921, 1925]) was very close to that
of the Prague school and Leonard Bloomfield, and rather distant
from that of Chomsky and Halle.

     21. Cf. especially Jakobson and Halle (1956). Recognition of
phonemes as consisting of bundles of distinctive features (phonological components) etc.) is of course much older than Jakobson; cf.,
for instance, Sapir [1925], Bloomfield [1933a:77-80] — especially
p. 79, where Bloomfield speaks of "a minimum unit of distinctive
sound-features, a phoneme" -- and Z. S. Harris (1944), to say nothing of more remote predecessors.

     22. E.g. by Joos (1948, 1957).

     23. Cf., for instance, such standard discussions as those of
Bloomfield (1933b); Baugh (1935:§§56-66, 142-144, 157-165, 211-
220); Francis (1958:185, 191-200).

     24. Hence the ridiculous spectacle of purists declaiming a-
gainst all non-Anglo-Saxon elements in English, and at the same
time using (inevitably) such words as *use*, *chief*, etc., in their
discussions.

     25. Cf. Bloomfield (1933b).

     26. Including words which may have come to English as borrow-
ings from French or other Romance languages, but preserving Latin
phonological features rather than showing popular developments
(e.g. *fragile* vs. *frail*).

     27. A further note on the competence-versus-performance de-
bate is in order here. Each speaker's competence is part of his
own personal make-up, not of some imaginary "langue" of a superor-
ganic kind existing outside the individual speakers (cf. Hall
[1968a: ch. 2]). It follows that no-one can set up rules, formulae, or any other kind of abstractions which are presumed to be
valid for all the speakers of a community, so that variations from
the rules can be stigmatized as "ungrammatical" and dismissed from
one's consideration (e.g. *permít* as a noun; cf. below in the main
text). It follows, also, that text-frequency is as important as
list-frequency, if not more so [it now seems to me much more important — RAHjr., 1985], in deciding what does and does not belong to any speaker's competence.

     28. That Scottish and perhaps speakers of other dialects of
English have [x] as an actual sound, and that this is a survival of
an earlier situation in which most or all varieties of English had
a phoneme /x/, is not germane to the description of modern standard
British or American English. Excessive generalization obscures the
essential fact of human language that varieties of speech are not
only similar, but also different in their structure.

     29. Often humorously spelt *mewel*, as in P. G. Wodehouse's
Big Money (ch. 8): "You'll have to carry the stuff over the moun-
tains on the backs of mewels". What, incidentally, are we to do
with *newel* (*post*): is this to be interpreted as /nule/?

     30. The term used by Esper (1968:222) in his accurate charac-

terization of Chomskyan methods.

31. As has been alleged by Keyser (1963), Wagner (1969), King (1969), and a number of others following in Chomsky's and Halle's train.

32. Many naïve observers tend, if anything, to exaggerate the irregularities and inconsistencies of English spelling, so that it has been necessary to argue (as I did, for instance, in Hall [1961]) for its essential, though by no means complete, regularity.

33. Cf. Hockett (1961); Hall (1972c).

34. This is not to deny that, especially in learnèd words, the position of stress is often (not always) determined by the formative elements, especially affixes; this was recognized by Bloomfield (1933b) for English, and stated extensively for Italian by myself (Hall [1971a:ch. 6]).

35. For an extensive discussion of Saltarelli's analysis of Italian phonology, cf. Hall (1972c).

36. The raised letter "x" in the transcription of Italian words stands for syntactic doubling; cf. Hall (1971a:§ 1.622).

37. Some, indeed, would object to even the most transparently obvious semantic and phonetic resemblances being taken into account, unless they correspond to historical developments; cf. the anguished protests of Pisani (1971). [For this whole matter, cf. now Hall (1977b].)

38. This insistence on a single "underlying representation" for each morpheme is a manifestation, on the phonological level, of the "passionate desire for unity, for complete logic and explanation" which Steiner (1971:125) has seen in Chomsky's over-all out-look, and on which he has commented "Unreason and the obstinate disorder of local fact may prove resistant to the claims of either political issues or formal logic" (ibid.).

39. One way out of this problem is, of course, to deny (as does, for instance, Anttila [1972:6]) that suppletion exists, i.e. that morphs can be grouped together under the same morpheme unless there is a phonological resemblance between them. However, when every-one, naïve native speakers and linguistic analysts alike, recognizes the semantic identity and complementary distribution in such sets as *go* (pres.) ∿ *went* (past), it would seem unrealistic to deny that the relationship is the same as that prevailing in sets of phonologically similar alternants such as *buy* ∿ *bought*, *eat* ∿ *ate*, *cook* ∿ *cooked*, etc.

40. Especially in failing to recognize the difference between inversion-liaison (as in /dontil/ *donne-t-il?* 'does he give?' versus /ildonăkor/ *il donne encore* 'he still gives', which is phrasally conditioned, and the kind of liaison which does not depend on inversion and is inflectionally determined, as in /dortil/ *dort-il?* 'does he sleep?' and /ildortăkor/ *il dort encore*. In these two last examples, liaison is obligatory in the former and optional (in very conservative usage, e.g. in reading poetry aloud) in the latter.

I have not included any discussion of Chomsky and Halle's treatment of Slavic phonology (1968:420-430), because it is outside my field of specialization. However, cf. the observations of Anderson (1969:572-573, n. 33) concerning their analysis: "Unfortunately, the set of correspondences they choose to account for is so radically simplified as to bear only a superficial resemblance to the Slavic data".

41. As observed by Esper (1968:220-221) and others.

42. For these last-mentioned, cf. Hall (1944b,1950a).

43. In addition to Hammarström (1971), we may mention such other recent studies as Buyssens (1969), Coseriu (1969), Collinder (1970), and (for the by now notorious "Cartesian linguistics") Aarsleff (1970, 1971).

REVIEW OF HOCKETT, *THE STATE OF THE ART*

(Italian version in Ricerche Linguistiche 6.313-336 [1974])

CHARLES F. HOCKETT. The state of the art.[1] The Hague - Paris,
Mouton, 1968. (Janua Linguarum, Series Minor, no. 73).
Pp. 123.

From 1957 onward, the current of "transformational-generative"
grammar (TGG) has steadily grown stronger, under the impulse given
by A. N. Chomsky in a series of books and articles.[2] Until recently, American criticism of the "transformationalist" approach
has been rather muted;[3] in Europe, on the other hand, there have
been several quite severe critiques.[4] Hockett's book is the
first thorough critical evaluation published by an American linguist. His objections are such as to deserve a detailed exposition; but to understand both TGG doctrines and H's criticisms, we
must back-track in time and review the history of linguistics in A-
merica since Sapir and Bloomfield.[5]

Between 1920 and 1950, the two most outstanding American linguists were undoubtedly Edward Sapir (1884-1939) and Leonard Bloomfield (1887-1949). Both were of German Jewish origin, and both received their original training in Indo-European linguistics, turning later to the study of less well-known languages. Sapir worked
on a number of American Indian languages, whereas Bloomfield analysed first Tagálog and then the Algonquian languages.[6] Each published a book on general linguistics entitled *Language*, Sapir in
1921 and Bloomfield in 1933.[7] In their approach to language, in
the narrow sense, they were very close: they both wished to make
linguistics a science; both were masters of descriptive and structural linguistics; and both were in close touch with the major European developments of their day, especially with the Prague school.
(but neither was a slavish follower of any European group). At the
same time, both were highly competent in historical linguistics, to
which they applied the methods and insights of synchronic analysis.
They were persuaded of the rightness of the principle of regularity
in phonetic change, which both Sapir and Bloomfield had applied successfully to families of American Indian languages.[8] They disagreed, however, on the relation of linguistics to neighboring
fields. Both considered it a branch of cultural anthropology, but
Sapir was given to (often rather daring) speculations on the psychological, philosophical and even aesthetic aspects of human language, whereas Bloomfield, though not denying their existence,[9]
was much more cautious with regard to them.

Up to 1940, and especially in the thirties, linguistics was

in poor shape in North America, with few professors and even fewer
students. Even before the United States' entry into the Second
World War, however, the need for teaching foreign languages rapidly
and effectively contributed to a revival of interest in linguistics,
both theoretical and applied. For young linguists in those days,
who had to face the problem of analysing and describing little
known or unknown languages, Bloomfield's book and teachings were
much more helpful than were Sapir's. This was also the experience
of many missionaries (both Protestant and Catholic) who desired to
apply the findings of linguistics to translating the Bible into in-
digenous languages.[10] Bloomfield himself was firmly opposed to the
establishment of "schools" and to *odium theologicum*;[11] nevertheless,
many observers thought they saw in his pupils and followers a compact school, which, however, in fact never existed.[12] In actuality, not many American linguists who came to maturity between 1935
and 1050 remained wholly uninfluenced by Bloomfield. His influence was exerted primarily through his book *Language*, but there
was such a great diversity in the characters and the attitudes of
individual scholars that they can by no means all be lumped together under the label of "post-Bloomfieldians" or "neo-Bloomfieldians" without distinction. They must be divided into at least four
groups, whom we shall temporarily term "A", "B", "C", and "D", and
whose chief members we shall list in alphabetical order:

A

Frederick B. Agard
William M. Austin, Jr.
Bernard Bloch
Franklin Edgerton
Zellig S. Harris
Charles F. Hockett
John Kepke
Norman A. McQuown
Henry Lee Smith, Jr.
George L. Trager

B

Ben Elson
Sarah Gudschinsky
Robert E. Longacre
Howard McKaughan
Eugene A. Nida
Velma B. Pickett
Eunice V. Pike
Evelyn Pike
Kenneth Lee Pike
Richard S. Pittman
William L. Wonderly

C

George M. Bolling
Yuen Ren Chao
Murray B. Emeneau
Charles C. Fries
E. Adelaide Hahn
Robert A. Hall, Jr.
Archibald A. Hill
Fred W. Householder, Jr.
Hans Kurath
Winfred P. Lehmann
Albert B. Marckwardt
Raven I. McDavid, Jr.
William G. Moulton
Thomas A. Sebeok
Edgar H. Sturtevant
W. Freeman Twaddell
Charles F. Voegelin
Ralph L. Ward

D

Manuel Andrade
Dwight L. Bolinger
Eric P. Hamp
Einar Haugen
R.-M. S. Heffner

Harry Hoijer
Roland G. Kent
C. E. Parmenter
Morris Swadesh

It would be fair to say, I believe, that the members of all
four of these groups regarded linguistics as a scientific discipline, to which it is possible to apply inductive method (deriving
theories from observed and observable facts; proceeding by hypotheses and verification, and discarding unsustained hypotheses; using
experimental methods as far as possible; and maintaining objectivity and an impersonal attitude.[13] The members of the first three
groups came, sooner or later, to recognize Bloomfield's *Language*
as the best exemplification, to date, of scientific methods in linguistics. The members of the fourth group, on the other hand, did
not share this view. (They were, however, not hostile on this account towards those of the first-mentioned three groups; in those
times, almost all American linguists enjoyed friendly relationships
with each other.) Of group "D", some belonged to an older generation (Andrade, Heffner, Kent, Parmenter); some were more closely
connected with Sapir and his out-look (Hoijer, Swadesh); and some
had come to linguistics by other paths (Bolinger, Hamp, Haugen).[14]

The term "post-" or "neo-Bloomfieldians" has been applied,
loosely, to the members of the first three groups, which we have
set up separately because of their divergent view-points. (Until
the 1960's, there was never any orthodox approach imposed from either within or without.[15]) In group "A" I have listed those who,
as often happens between teacher and disciples, were "plus roya-
listes que le roi", carrying certain of Bloomfield's teachings to
an extreme. He had been skeptical with regard to certain tendencies which he considered unscientific — for instance, "psychologizing" linguistics, and especially the variety of "mentalism" in
which the existence of a factor called "mind" or "spirit" is assumed to exist, invisible, inaccessible to observation, but by definition essential to analysis, and to which any phenomenon can be
ascribed when it cannot be explained in any other way.[16] With regard to meaning, Bloomfield never denied either its existence or
its importance, but considered it relatively inaccessible to scientific investigation, because the meaning of every linguistic
phenomenon necessarily includes, for each speaker or listener, the
totality of his or her previous experiences in connection with the
phenomenon that the linguistic forms refer to. For this reason,
Bloomfield considered it preferable to begin the study of linguistic phenomena from their formal side, which is more immediately
accessible, and then to pass later to the semantic side.[17]

For the members of our group "A" and their pupils, however,
Bloomfield's diffidence in these respects became almost an absolute
taboo, with regard to psychology and meaning, and also what came to
be called "mixing of levels". According to some (especially G. L.
Trager), phonology, morphology and syntax formed three absolutely
independent levels, to be kept wholly separate in both analysis and
presentation. The linguist, in this approach, was obliged to complete the study and description of phonology before starting in on
morphology, and this latter was to serve as an indispensable base
for work on syntax. In descriptive technique, it was fashionable

to favor a purely synchronic type of description, from which was
excluded even the notion of "grammatical process", which was dear
to Sapir and to his mentor in the description of American Indian
languages, but which was not rejected by Bloomfield. The two re-
sulting models were often called, respectively, "item-and-arrangement" (IA) and "item-and-process" (IP).[18] Both were based on fictions,[19] but the IA model gave results which were comparable to
anatomical sketches, in their apparent lack of life; furthermore,
the IA technique often required very artificial manipulations in
order to avoid the slightest suggestion of movement as the linguist passed from one item to another.[20] At certain universities
and at the summer-sessions of the Linguistic Institute, the prestige and the influence of our group "A" was very great, exercised
chiefly through their text-books.[21] These books had and still
have great merits, on account of which they soon became widely
used, replacing others less advanced. Nevertheless, they incor-
porated the above-mentioned shortcomings, which rendered them more
vulnerable to the reaction to be discussed below.

We must not forget, however, that our group "A" was far from
constituting a majority, even of "Bloomfieldians" in general. In
group "B" I have listed the names of those linguists who, under the
leadership of Kenneth L. Pike and Eugene A. Nida, directed the activities of the Summer Institute of Linguistics. The text-books[22]
written by these linguists were used in the courses given at the
Summer Institute of Linguistics, and also in many of those of the
Linguistic Institute and other schools. The aim of this group was
to use linguistics in preparing translations of the Bible, i.e.
with a very practical purpose in mind. This concern aided them to
avoid becoming dogmatic on matters of linguistic analysis, since
they had to deal with languages of widely differing structure, and
also led them to accord full and thorough consideration to problems
of meaning, while also avoiding "separation of levels". Nida devoted his prime attention to the problems of semantic and cultural
equivalence.[23] Together with Fries, Pike protested, even as early
as the 1940's, against any excessive rigidity in the exclusion of
morpho-syntactic considerations from phonological analysis,[24] and
against the treatment of any phonological system as if it were
wholly monolithic.[25]

Under group "C" are listed the members of the largest group,
those who, while recognizing the importance of Bloomfield's work,
admiring it and deriving great profit from it, nevertheless were
never slavish nor fanatical followers of his.[26] For completeness'
sake, we should mention the names of certain refugee scholars who,
in one way or another, were similar to this group in their attitudes and contributed greatly to the development of American linguistics while sacrificing nothing of their professional individu-
ality: Paul Garvin, Henry M. Hoenigswald, Henry and Renée Kahane,
Ernst Pulgram, and (perhaps to a lesser extent) Yakov Malkiel.

It was clear that, from certain points of view, the approach of

the "type A" Bloomfieldians was unsatisfactory, because their efforts to be scientific and rigorous rendered them only rigid and
schematic. One cannot eliminate meaning from linguistics, even in
theory. The separation of levels can be analytically useful, to a
certain extent, provided its fictitious nature is recognized: in
speaking and listening, every-one is active on all levels at the
same time, and it is unreasonable to suppose that speakers keep
them separate in every-day life. These objections had been raised
well before 1957, but the time had come for a more wide-spread reaction, with the publication of Chomsky's *Syntactic Structures*.

In this book and in the others listed above (note 2), Chomsky
reacted strongly against the positions of our group "A". He in-
sisted, however, on ascribing those positions to all his predecessors and even to Bloomfield himself.[27] The general attitude of
Chomsky and his school (and here we must, unfortunately, speak spe-
cifically of a "school") has been termed "rejectionism",[28] because
the Chomskyites rejected virtually all the methods practised in
linguistics up to 1960, and thereby denied the cumulative nature of
science. In his theory of linguistic analysis, Chomsky returned to
apriorism and rationalism, preferring the deductive approach, in
which one first sets up a theory and then fits into it whatever
facts can be forced to fit, and neglecting any that do not. Objectivity is replaced by subjectivity, and observation by intuition.
Linguistics ceases to be an independent science, and is brought
back to the status of a humble hand-maid of philosophy and psychology, which it had occupied before its emancipation at the hands of
the linguists of the nineteenth century and the first half of the
twentieth. All scientific work has to rest on the establishment of
analytical units; these, in the Chomskyan approach, are replaced by
endless sequences of rules.[29]

In the presentation of linguistic material, Chomsky abandons
the customary order of phonology — morphology — syntax, to follow
the inverse procedure, beginning with syntax and deriving morphology from it, as the "realization" of syntactic combinations,[30] and
relegating phonology to the last place, as a mere physical manifestation of the abstract models of morphology.[31] The "separation of
levels" is wholly rejected, so that the introduction of morphosyn-
tactic considerations is considered justified in the establishment
of a phonemic inventory. A concrete example from Italian: the contrast between forms like *càpitano* 'they arrive' and *capitàno* 'cap-
tain' is rejected as a criterion for regarding stress as phonemically significant. Why? — because the former is a verb-form, and
the latter a noun, and we are told that the place of the stress is
predictable in terms of the morphological categories to which these
contrasting forms belong.[32] "Biuniqueness", i.e. exact correspond-
ence between a phoneme and its allophones, is abandoned, because
the phonemes themselves are regarded as mere realizations of more
important elements which can have various representations on the
phonetic level. The phonemic level is no longer regarded as an
essential part of linguistic structure, because one "descends"

from morphology to the phonic level, directly from the supposed "underlying representation" of morphology, syntax and semantics to its incorporation in phonetic shape.

All this is justified by a contrast between "surface" and "deep" structure; the former, we are told, is simply a more or less distorted representation of the latter, which is the only true structure. Differences between languages, we are told, is due only to divergences between surface structures, i.e. in the way in which speech-communities give expression to the same universal concepts. How do we know that these universal concepts exist, and that they are the same for all humans? We assume it *a priori*, through our intuition, and because it "stands to reason" that it must be so. Chomsky has asserted many times, and his disciples have kept repeating *ad infinitum*, that all human languages have the same "deep structure", with a syntactic nucleus consisting of SUBJECT + PREDICATE, *in that order*. The task of the linguist is then, we are told, to discover in what way this universal "deep structure" is revealed in the various languages of mankind. It is easy to see that we are very close to the aprioristic rationalism of the so-called Port-Royal grammar (A. Arnauld and C. Lancelot's *Grammaire universelle et raisonnée* of 1660). Not surprisingly, Chomsky has claimed to discover, in Arnauld and Lancelot's work, an inspired precursor of his own theories.[33] Through this desire of attaining universality, the interest in language-universals has come again to the fore, in contrast to the lack of interest shown in them by those who, following Franz Boas,[34] had paid greater attention to the differences between linguistic structures. Such an interest, in what may possibly be wide-spread and even universal in human language, is in itself perfectly justified, and there had been a certain revival of interest in "universals" even before Chomsky's time.[35] In his approach, however, the linguist is led to believe that he or she can attain a knowledge of universals, not by paying attention to mere facts, but by starting from logic and by deducing therefrom, aprioristically, what the universals of human language must necessarily be.

Consequently, in the Chomskyan approach, linguistics ceases to be a science of investigation, in which the facts of human speaking are observed, examined, and classified, and studied in relation to other aspects of the activity of humans in their individual and social life. It becomes, instead, mere jugglery in the formulation of rules to express the relation between already-known facts, from any source whatsoever. Chomsky has repeatedly declared that the way in which the linguist obtains his data is unimportant, and that what matters is the "correctness" of his presentation of these data.[36] Hence the linguist's task is reduced to the excogitation of formulae so as to pass from an input to an out-put, exactly as is done in computer-programming. (It is not exact to say, as some have done,[37] that TGG originated in experience gained from computer-science and machine-translation; but it is beyond doubt that TGG was strongly influenced thereby, especially in treating humans

as if they were machines — neglecting culture entirely — and as
if their activities were determined wholly automatically.)

The formulae which the linguist excogitates to "generate" (only
in the logical sense) the sentences of a given language are expressed in rules. One of the most frequently given definitions of
an ideal grammar is that of M. Halle,[38] according to which it
should consist of a body of rules which permit the linguist to generate all the well-formed sentences, and only those, of a given
language, from a syntactic nucleus.

Central to this concept of grammar is the idea of "well-formed
sentences". There arises, in this way, the problem of "grammaticality", because certain utterances are to be considered well-formed
and others not. It has often been observed that Chomsky's original
notion, in his 1957 *Syntactic Structures*, that of a sharp opposition between sentences which were grammatical and those which were
not (and could hence easily be excluded from the linguist's consideration), is untenable.[39] What shall we say, for instance, about
an Italian sentence like this: *erano arrivati lassù un sacco di
gente* 'a whole bunch of people had arrived up there, lit. "had
arrived [m.pl.] up there a sack [m.sg.] of people [f.sg.]"', which
I heard from a native speaker of Italian in 1944, à propos of a
group of refugees from bombings? The sentence was uttered in a
conversation, its occurrence was not commented on, and it was,
therefore, accepted by the hearers of the utterance. This was obviously a case of *constructio ad sensum*, which is neither logical
nor "grammatical", but which pccurs all the time in normal every-
day speech. To save the concept of grammaticality, Chomsky and his
followers have tried to dilute it, setting up a distinction between
grammaticality and acceptability. In the instance just cited, the
utterance might be acceptable to all the listeners, but would nevertheless be permanently ungrammatical (a position opposite, therefore, to the well-known principle of law *communis error facit jus*).
In this way, the linguist's attention is steered away from a very
great part of our every-day linguistic activity, simply because it
does not conform to the pre-conceived notions of the TGG grammarian with regard to what his generative rules prescribe.[40]

To explain all the slips-of-the-tongue, anacoluthons, blends,
and other "ungrammatical" utterances which are so frequent in normal every-day speech, Chomskyan theory has recourse to another distinction, between "competence" and "performance". The former, we
are told, is the structure which is inherent in the linguistic
system, identical or nearly so for all men in its deep form, and
for a given language in its superficial form (a concept fairly
close to the Saussurean notion of *langue*). The latter, however,
is supposedly the momentary, transitory manifestation of the former in the act of speaking, and includes all individual variations
(Saussure's *parole*, in one of the senses of this much-discussed
concept). Variations from the norm which can be observed in
performance are supposedly all to be ascribed to various types of in-

terference (faulty memory, hesitation, nervousness, etc.) which
spoil the perfect realization of competence (which, by definition,
is without imperfections). Here we are back at the old Platonic
notion of linguistic structure as an ideal, realized in manifestations which are rendered imperfect only by external factors.[41]

The concept of "rule", too, is central in TGG theory. There
are two senses in which this term is used in linguistics:[42] that of
the transformation of an indicative into an imperative, and that of
an order given by some authority for correct behavior according to
some pre-established norm. The first use of this term is trivial,
since every observation of fact can be transformed into a command
(e.g. "Italians are in the habit of making a noun and its modifying
adjective agree, as in *belle ragazze* 'beautiful girls' if you
want to talk as the Italians do, make your nouns and their adjectives agree"). The second, on the other hand, implies the existence of some person or institution that has the right to give such
orders — and here we are right back at the seventeenth- and eighteenth-century notion of authoritarianism in language, whether it
be that of Malherbe-style *ipse dixit*, or that of a legally established authority like the Académie Française, or that of abstract
logic à la Port-Royal. In TGG, the rules — which are normally arrived at by logical procedures — have to be arranged in such an
order as to produce the desired result, proceeding from a more general rule to a more specific one. No other mechanism than that of
rules is recognized in the production of sentences — denying, for
instance, the existence or importance of analogy. In establishing
rules, and in determining the order in which they are to be applied, Chomskyan doctrine calls for mathematical and logical principles to be followed; for many, Chomsky's "mathematicization" of
linguistics has constituted a real and highly important "break-
through".[43]

At the same time, the Chomskyan conception of language still
separates linguistic structure sharply from meaning. The latter is
considered as a separate domain, with its own structure, whose elements can be set up, divided, and sub-divided in an aprioristic
fashion.[44] One of the favorite formulas of the Chomskyan school is
"grammar + semantics = linguistics". The neglect of the differences between the meaning of one syntactic or morphological construction and that of another leads TGG to regard as semantically
identical two or more structures which are, in fact, not identical,
e.g. active and passive. Thus, in (say) *the dog bites the man* and
the man is bitten by the dog, the event to which the two sentences
refer is the same, but the two sentences present it in two very
different lights, because of the different emphases placed on the
factors involved in the situation. Another consequence of this neglect of meaning is that Chomskyites confuse grammaticality and
sense, and often attach the label "ungrammatical" to utterances
which are simply nonsensical. Metaphor and humor are foreign to
the thought of transformationalists, so that they are unable to
consider as "grammatical" a sentence like *Last week I spent a year*

in Italy.

Not content with bringing about such a radical about-face in linguistics itself, Chomsky and his school have thought to extend their conclusions to neighboring fields, with regard to the relation of language to other types of human activity. It is affirmed that "deep structure" is innate in human beings, because — we are told — it is inconceivable that a child could learn, in a very short time after birth, such a complicated structure. Therefore, according to Chomsky, in a child's learning of language we behold, not a process of imitation and analogical extension of a set of habits, but the budding and flowering of an innate "competence". In the teaching of foreign languages, also, Chomskyan principles would reduce to a minimum the formation of phonetic, grammatical, and semantic habits which are different from those of the learner, substituting the learning of rules and the development of so-called "rule-governed behavior".

Underlying all this complex of dogmas — the great majority of which are promulgated *a priori* and regarded as articles of faith — is the belief that linguistic systems are well-defined, i.e. completely coherent, without "fuzzy edges", and therefore amenable to mathematical formulation. In this respect, Chomskyan doctrines are a reflection of the present-day vogue of mathematics,[45] and of the (highly doubtful) principle that sciences are to be evaluated according to the extent to which they can be organized on the basis of mathematical procedures. In its turn, this view depends on the presupposition that mathematics depends on logic, and that the development of mathematical formalisms can, therefore, take place according to the predetermined schemes of symbolic logic.

One might ask why TGG, together with all the philosophical, logical, and mathematical appurtenances of the "Chomskyan revolution", was able to spread so rapidly, not only in America, but also, up to a certain point, in Europe. There are several answers to this question. As we have already pointed out, the time was ripe, in America, for a reasonable reaction against the excesses of our "type-A" Bloomfieldians, but it was not necessary for all the others (of types "B" and "C"), and even Bloomfield himself,[46] to be dragged in. With the development of electronic computers and with interest in machine-translation, linguistics was invaded by a great number of persons (engineers, mathematicians, cyberneticians) who knew no linguistic system other than that of their native language (in general, English), and who were therefore unable to free themselves (nor did they know that they needed to free themselves) from all of our society's folk-lore concerning such matters as "correctness" in language. Many psychologists and philosophers, especially those of the "mentalist" variety, had felt shut out of a field which they had traditionally regarded as a fief of theirs, began again to intervene in linguistics under the aegis of a leader whose theories were much more in line with their prejudices than those of Bloomfield and his followers. Traditional grammarians, who had

REVIEW OF HOCKETT, THE STATE OF THE ART

felt their pride and their domination over the teaching of class-
room-grammar threatened, as a result of the frequent condemnations
of their doctrines (beginning with Fries [1925], an exposé of the
unfounded nature of traditional rules "governing" the use of the
English auxiliaries *shall* and *will*),[47] felt they had found an ally
in Chomsky and his aprioristic and authoritarian doctrines, which
seemed to confirm their views.[48] Finally, in sharp contrast with
the spirit of inter-generational amity which had prevailed earlier
(see above), during the 1960's the so-called "generation-gap" pre-
dominated, in which younger scholars rejected *a priori* any and every view held by their elders. Because of his political views —
which, from an objective point of view, should have found no place
in his scientific activity[49] — Chomsky became one of the idols of
certain extremist groups, a "guru" for true believers. This phenomenon contributed in large measure to his popularity with new-com-
ers to linguistics, in a purely irrational fashion.

After this long but necessary prologue, let us now turn to
Hockett's book. He himself had, at the outset, not been hostile to
Chomsky's new approach, despite the latter's unfavorable and arro-
gant review of Hockett's *Manual of Phonology*.[50] For a time, also
because of his well-known interest in mathematical and algebraical
linguistics,[51] H was persuaded of the essential rightness of
Chomskyan position. The high point of what H now terms his "eu-
phoria", i.e. infatuation, for Chomsky's theories was reached in
his presidential address to the Linguistic Society of America,[52]
in which he speaks of four "break-throughs" in linguistics, the
last of which he considered Chomsky's "mathematicization" to be.
Later, however, H became persuaded that such a mathematicization is
not possible, and that Chomsky's position is untenable because it
has no base in the nature of linguistic structure itself. The
book under review is a discussion of the "state of the art" of
present-day linguistics, aimed at demonstrating the unfounded nature of Chomsky's doctrines.

The State of the Art is divided into six chapters, of which the
first, "The Background" (9-37), is a summary of the development of
linguistic theory, principally in the United States, from 1900 to
1950. H discusses first the opposition of synchrony and diachrony
(10-18), including under this heading also the presumed rigidity
of linguistic systems and the notion of *langue* as a social norm,
recognizing the (at least partly) erroneous basis of the Saussurean
and Bloomfieldian approach, with its excessively sharp separation
between description and history. He then passes to the delimita-
tion and structure of grammar, in an essentially autobiographical
sub-chapter (19-50), describing his own reactions and those of the
other members of our "group A" towards certain divisions which
Bloomfield established, especially the relation betwen phonology,
morphology and syntax. H now recognizes that the parallelism which
he and Z. S. Harris set up between phonological and morphological
structure was not justified, inasmuch as each of the two levels has
a different type of organization. In the third sub-chapter (31-32),

H describes the situation as of ca. 1950. enumerating (31-32) three
ideas which were then current: (1) that linguistic systems were rigid and that, in describing them, change not only could but should
be left out of account; (2) that the "IA" model (see above) was valid for both phonology and morphology; and (3) that grammar and semantics could and should be kept separate. H now recognizes that
"we" (i.e. himself and the others of our group "A") were wrong on
all three of these points, which should be abandoned in favor of
the previously prevalent positions.

    H notes with approval (34) the practical usefulness of syntac-
tic transformations in descriptions of structure, and that of or-
dered rules in syntax and morphemics, but rightly observes that
these are "largely a corrective to certain temporary extremists
of the 1940's" (he might have added "of a certain narrow group")
"a reintroduction, with improvements and under a new name, of
certain useful features of the Bloomfieldian and Sapirian view of
language, that we had set aside". Discussing the relationship of
Chomsky to his predecessors, particularly Z. S. Harris (who was his
mentor at the University of Pennsylvania), H perceives a correlation between the narrowness of Harris's view of linguistics
(which would have reduced it to an empty, sterile game of formalisms) and Chomsky's reaction in search of a broader view-point:
"Lacking any explicit guidance as to where to turn for a broad-
ened basis for linguistic theory, Chomsky was forced on his own
resources and taste, and turned towards the abstract fields of logic, mathematics, and philosophy, rather than to science" (36).
But, according to H, the Chomskyan theory of language, "which differs strikingly from any proposed by linguists or philologists,
or by psychologists or philosophers, during the last hundred years
or more" (36), rejects the second of the three erroneous views
discussed above, but incorporates uncritically the first and the
third, which constitute capital defects of his approach (36-37).

    The second chapter, "The Chomskyan orientation" (38-43), con-
sists of an enumeration of nineteen points which constitutes a
summary of Chomsky's views.[53] We shall summarize them very briefly, indicating the main content of each point:

    (1) the novelty of the vast majority of the sentences pro-
duced by any user (= speaker-hearer) of a language or heard by
him or her;
    (2) the infinite set of possible sentences;
    (3) the competence of the user (= his or her knowledge of
the grammar of the language);
    (4) the theory of performance, which is of necessity secon-
dary with respect to competence;
    (5) the ideal speaker-listener;
    (6) the mental nature of the user's competence;
    (7) the irrelevance of probabilistic considerations for
competence.
    (8) the distinction between grammatical and non-grammatical

sentences, which applies to competence, not to performance (as
distinct from the degree of acceptability of an actually performed utterance;
    9. Meaningfulness, which, like grammaticality, pertains to
competence;
    10. The well-definedness of the grammar of a language (in the
mathematical sense), characterizing an infinite number of well-
formed sentences;
    11. The absence of a known algorithm for computing or "dis-
covering" the grammar of a language;
    12. The existence of an innate system in the child for pro-
ducing an infinitely large number of grammars, and the innate ability to choose among them a correct grammar for the language of
one's speech-community;
    13. The equivalence of a "general grammar" with an explicit
formulation of the child's innate grammar-producing system;
    14. The "well-definedness" of this innate system;
    15. The existence of three distinct components in the grammar
of every language — syntax, phonology, and semantics;
    16. The descriptive adequacy of a grammar for any language,
to be determined by its conformity to general grammar (no. 13);
    17. The search for a correct general linguistic theory, con-
forming to the innate language-system of the child (no. 12);
    18. The irrelevance of the use made of the language by its
users, for the grammar of the language, i.e. for the ideal competence of the ideal speaker-listener's competence;
    19. Linguistic change regarded as a shift from one grammar
(of the set of grammars of all "possible" human languages [cf. no.
12]) to another (presumably similar) one.

    In the following chapter, "Well-Defined and Ill-Defined" (44-
52), H examines in detail the proposition set forth in point 10
(above), and quotes two sentences from Chomsky (1965:8): "Although
it was well understood (in the nineteenth century) that linguistic
processes are in some sense 'creative', the technical devices for
expressing a system of recursive processes were simply not available until much more recently. In fact, a real understanding of
how a language can (in Humboldt's words) 'make infinite use of finite means' has developed only within the last thirty years, in the
course of studies in the foundations of mathematics". To refute
Chomskyan dogma on this point, H discusses and exemplifies the
principle of computability and unsolvability.[54] According to this
principle, a well-defined system is one of whatever type (physical,
conceptual, mathematical) that can be characterized completely and
exactly by means of functions which can be effectively calculated
by an algorithm. If a system is not completely characterizable in
such terms, it is ill-defined, and consequently cannot be described
in the mathematical terms necessary for computation (45). As examples of well-defined systems, H adduces and discusses the infinite
series of integers (45-46); the decimal approximations up to n for
π (3.1, 3.14, 3.142, ... n) (46-47); the game of chess (49-50);
American base-ball (51-52); and the series of chemical formulae for

all possible hydrocarbons (54-55). As examples of ill-defined systems, on the other hand, he cites American foot-ball (47-48); mid-
dle-class American table-manners, as described by Boas[55] (51-52);
any physical system (52-54); and the hydrocarbons themselves, as
contrasted with their descriptive formulae (55). In each of the
second set of examples, there is an indeterminacy which stands in
the way of an exact description of the system involves, and which
inevitably introduces a vagueness, a "fuzziness", which can be gotten rid of only by arbitrary decisions. Hockett also notes
(52-54) that one should not confuse stability (which can character-
ize a physical system over a shorter or longer period of time) with
well-definedness.

Now, what are the characteristics of linguistic systems, with
regard to the problem of computability and unsolvability? To which
class of science does linguistics belong — to that of empirical
sciences, like chemistry, or to that of formal disciplines like logic and mathematics? H takes up this problem in Chapter 4, "The
Status of Languages" (56-59), suggesting that the only well-defined
systems are those invented *ex novo* by human intelligence, like the
games of chess and base-ball, formal systems of mathematics and logic, and perhaps also some legal and theological systems. He examines the possible ways in which, if we admit that linguistic systems are well-defined, they could have originated, either from other well-defined systems, or from ill-defined systems; and he shows
that one could hypothesize no other well-defined origin than from
some fundamental well-defined system, non-physical and existing
permanently as a parallel to the physical universe. Such a hypothesis would not be in accord with scientific principles, and
would hardly be verifiable by means of techniques of experiment and
observation. H concludes that the problem can have only an either-
or answer: either linguistic systems are well-defined, or they are
ill-defined. If we assume that they are the former, the problem a-
rises of showing how they could have originated in an ill-defined
universe, except by assuming a metaphysical origin (and thereby a-
bandoning scientific method). If, on the other hand, we consider
them ill-defined, another problem arises: that of showing how ordinary language, used in certain ways, could have given rise to well-
defined systems like mathematics and logics. Chomsky, H says, has
chosen the first of the two answers just out-lined. H, on the other hand, chooses the second, saying

> With no hesitation whatsoever, I answer that linguistics
> is an empirical science; that "conclusions" reached about
> language on any other basis are worthy of scientific con-
> sideration only as hypotheses; and that even the very spe-
> cial communicative-symbolic behavior of logicians and ma-
> thematicians can be observed and described from the empi-
> rical point of view of science (without in the slightest
> challenging the worthiness of their activity). This an-
> swer is not a matter of taste, but of definition and of
> fact.

In the following two chapters, H continues and develops his argumentation, demolishing Chomsky's theories and then proposing a solution of his own for the problem.   In Chapter Five, "The Chomskyan View Dissected" (60-87), H takes up the nineteen points enumerated in his Chapter Three, in the same order.   He admits the rightness of the first point; considers the sixth irrelevant (because it contains only a definition, not an assertion); and rejects all the others.   Since linguistic systems are ill-defined, one cannot speak (point 2) of either infinite or finite series, since there is no definable limit for "the series of all possible sentences" of a language.   One can, by means of approximations (and, therefore, omitting certain aspects of what is being studied), treat an ill-defined system as if it were well-defined.   But, H observes (63), the aspects of linguistic systems which are omitted in this way are the most important characteristics of human language, inasmuch as they are the source of the possibility of forming new utterances (and, we might add, of adapting them to new situations and hence of their changing).   In Chomsky's procedures, H criticizes especially his ambiguous use of terms, e.g. the use of English *know* in two senses, 'to know how to' do something, and 'to have knowledge of' something (62-63).[56] If some-one 'knows' how to talk, i.e. has the habit of talking,[57] this does not mean that he has even the slightest analytical knowledge thereof; but Chomsky, passing (without the reader's being aware of the shift) from one of these meanings to the other, furnishes a perfect example of what H calls "Tarzan thinking" (63): "one grabs onto a vine (a word) at one tree (meaning) and leaves it only after it has swung to another tree".

According to H (67-70), Chomsky continues the fundamental error of the "post-Bloomfieldians" of our group "A", and especially of Z. S. Harris (but not of Bloomfield himself) in separating grammar and meaning.   On the other hand, H and almost all other non-TGG linguists now recognize that meaning cannot be separated from linguistic structure, since every morphological element and every syntactic element has a meaning of its own.   He remarks (71) that in linguistic structure we must recognize two unequal parts: the phonological system on the one hand, and on the other the extremely complex arrangements of the phonological material and their meanings.   This latter part includes both grammar and meaning at the same time, "the way in which a given language analyses the world".   Chomsky not only continues this unjustified separation between grammar and meaning, but adds thereto two further errors of his own (72-74).   In the first place, the Chomskyan definition of "meaningfulness" derives, not from esxperience, but from the logical notion of "truth-value", which has practically nothing to do with ordinary utterances (72-73).   Bivalent logic, in which there are only two values, "true" and "false", although it may suffice for a well-defined system, has no place in every-day human linguistic activity, in which the truth or falsity of an utterance has nothing to do with its abstract semantic function.[58] In the second place, Chomsky ascribes grammaticality and meaningfulness to competence, not performance. In this way, he protects it from being refuted by any empirical evidence, since competence, in the Chomskyan sense, is discovered, not by observation, but by aprioristic ratiocination. On the other hand, H says (73-74):

> For those of us whose principles forbid such escapism, grammaticality and meaningfulness, separable or not, must be sought within actual performance.
>
> The basic assumption has to be that *if something is in fact said in a language, it is allowed by the patterns of the language* — even if we fail to "understand" it or are unable to parse it. [Italics in the original.]

Otherwise we run the risk (as happened with Chomsky) of falling back into the futile purism of academics and school-marms, which is neither subtle enough nor clear-sighted enough to achieve an understanding of linguistic structure and meaning.

H does not deny the usefulness of the concept of the "ideal speaker" (66), provided its fictive and imaginary nature is recognized, but he suggests that we should speak, rather, of the "average" or "typical" user of a language. The ideal competence of the ideal user, however, and therefore also "correct grammar" (for either a given language or human language as a whole), are simply non-existent (76-77), and therefore can never be anything but a snipe-hunt. Chomsky's and his followers' refusal to admit the relevance of empirical evidence[59] is condemned by H, who rightly insists that the methods used in discovery and analysis of data are never foreign to scientific work. H recognizes the merits of some transformationalists' contributions, but states that "their contributions are despite, not because of Chomsky's antiscientific bias" (79).

That the child has a special aptitude for learning to speak, is not a new discovery: both genetic inheritance and the human condition (i.e. social life and culture) are necessary. But, starting from an aprioristic point of view, Chomsky has attacked eighteenth-century "scientific naturalism", advocating a return to seventeeth-century rationalism, so as to consider "deep structure" as innate.[60] H calls the Chomskyan expression of this view "weirdly misleading" (79), and observes that "the alternative to his 'rationalist' views is not eighteenth-century 'scientific naturalism', but twentieth-century empirical science" (80). In fact, if it is stripped of its metaphysical content, and if it is expressed in more exact terms, the Chomskyan doctrine boils down simply to the observation that the human capacity to speak is innate, but that the form which this capacity takes (i.e. competence in a non-Chomskyan sense) inevitably varies according to the speech-community into which the speaker is born. This is nothing new; it was formulated by Dante many centuries before Chomsky, in the famous verses:

Opera naturale è ch'uom favella;
Ma così o così, Natura lascia
Poi fare a voi, secondo che v'abbella

'It is a work of Nature [i.e. of the way he is made] that man
speaks; but whether this way or that, Nature leaves it up to you,
as pleases you best' (*Paradiso* 26.130-132).

In the last section of Chapter V, H reproves Chomsky for having
neglected all the progress made in historical linguistics in the
nineteenth century (81-83). For the "regularist" principle[61] and
for analogy, TGG substitutes a whirligig of rules, which afford no
insight into the possibility of change in a linguistic system,
since they are not open-ended. For H, on the other hand, "a language is a kind of system in which *every actual utterance*, whether
spoken aloud or merely thought to oneself, at once and the same
time by and large *conforms* to (or *manifests*) the system, and *changes* the system, however slightly"(83) (italics in the original).
At the end of the chapter (85-87), H describes an imaginary variant
of chess: a whole community spends all its available time in play-
ing, without either explicit or implicit rules, but with a tacit
and changeable consensus on permissibile moves, so that any move
can become permissible provided the community accepts it. In such
a game there would be vague notions of fairness and correctness,
different schools and "authorities", and there would be no clear
definition of unfair play. This game, which H terms "sandlot
chess", "is not very much like a language. But it is much more
like a language than is real chess" (87).

In the last chapter, "What Do We Know?" (88-118), H sets forth
his own views on the characteristics of human language, from a constructive view-point. In the first part, "The Openness of Language"
(89-99), he examines the mechanisms whereby a speaker can produce
new utterances, structurally different from those which are normal
in his or her speech-community. He suggests that, in the production of such "wrong" utterances, which deviate from the norm, there
are three basic factors: analogy, blending, and "editing" (essentially the revision either of what one is planning to say or, on
occasion, of what one has already started to say). The second
part, "Quotation and Dequotation" (99-109), is a presentation of
certain ways in which a speaker furnishes his or her listeners with
a commentary on what he or she has said, especially humorously
(e.g. laughing at an anacoluthon), but also by hypostasis, i.e.
quoting a linguistic form for further discussion (e.g. *"John" is
a proper noun*).

Finally, in the third part of the chapter, "The Linguistic
Foundations of Mathematics" (104-108), H shows that mathematics and
logic have their roots in the essential characteristics of linguistic structure, not vice versa. Human language permits us to speak
of many things at the same time; to say things which are false[62]
or possibly inexact; to ask for the identity of a specific thing;

to make statements about things which probably do not exist (e.g. an albino moose); to invent short and useful names; and to count. H traces all the characteristics of mathematical discourse to these properties of language and from certain uses of graphemic systems (which, in their turn, are derived from speech). The extension of mathematical concepts to infinity is made possible by endocentric constructions, of a type common in linguistic structures (106-109). The well-defined character of mathematics can have its origin in an ill-defined structure if we pretend that limitations on the repetition of an endocentric construction do not exist (110). In the rest of the chapter (111-117), H shows that the foundations of mathematics are not to be sought (as is often asserted) in logic, but that those of both mathematics and logic are to be found in every-day use of language. Only by using an artificial use of language, from which, by a fiction, have been excluded all the most essential and vital features of normal language, can stability (which incorporates the possibility of innovation) be established (116). In this way, H says (118), Bloomfield's dictum is vindicated (1933a:512): "The use of numbers is characteristic of speech-activity at its best. Who would want to live in a world of pure mathematics? Mathematics is merely the best that language can do".

After these criticisms — strong but justified — of the bases of Chomskyan theory, all that remains valid in Chomsky's doctrines is a few practical aspects. Transformations are a useful means of formulating certain grammatical relationships, especially in the structure of subordinate clauses and of elliptical constructions; but they are neither the only means nor, in many instances, the best. It is also possible that some languages may be more easily formulated in transformational terms than others — especially those whose elements come one after another in more or less linear sequence, as do those of English. With the current rage for transformational formulations, there is a great risk — which has already been noticed from the very beginning[63] — that an English model may be forced onto the grammar of all the other languages of the world, as, for instance, when we are told that "deep structure" must necessarily have at its centre the sequence SUBJECT + PREDICATE, in that order (cf. above), as in English and French. In this, TGG simply repeats the mistake of the seventeenth- and eighteenth-century grammarians who forced the structural categories of Latin onto all languages, including newly discovered "primitive" tongues.

Hockett's book is not free of faults, as when, for instance, he asserts that "Meanings are things and situations, or kinds of things and situations" (75). No: we should not confuse reference and sense. The things or the situations to which a given linguistic phenomenon refers are its "referents"; its sense, on the other hand, is the correlation betwen the linguistic form(s) and its or their referents. This is how it is possible, with a tighter or looser correlation, for the meaning (= sense + referent) of a

construction or a word to be precise or imprecise, clear or confused, according to the degree of correlation existing between
form and referent in the "mind" of the speaker. Nevertheless,
this monograph is a useful resource in opposing the "Chomskyan
revolution" — which is, in fact, not a revolution but a counter-
revolution, a kind of "Boxer rebellion",[64] whose aim is that of
expelling from the realm of grammatical tradition all the "foreign
devils" of scientific method, and which has prospered for the various reasons mentioned earlier. There are also more superficial
aspects which must be combatted, such as insistence on formulation
in terms of rules (which H characterizes [87] as "a misleading,
overly cumbersome, and [in some circles] dishonestly prestigious
substitute for the simpler traditional terminology"); unjustified
emphasis on premature generalizations, based only on a few European
languages; and the use of terms with unscientific emotional connotations.[65] But only if the principles advocated by Hockett are taken as basic, and only if linguistics is regarded as a social science, a kind of bridge between cultural anthropology and the humanities (instead of a humble hand-maiden of aprioristic logic), can
linguistics be brought back to its proper path, which is that of
scientific study of human beings' activity when they speak and
listen.

NOTES

1.   After this review was written, an Italian translation by G.
R. Cardona, entitled *La linguistica americana contemporanea*, appeared (Bari: Laterza, 1970; Universale Laterza, no. 167). The
translation is, in general, very good, except for one fairly serious error, the use of *àbito* instead of *abitudine* to translate Eng.
habit.

2.   Among the books may be mentioned Chomsky (1957a) and the
naïve rave-review given it by his pupil R. B. Lees (1957); Chomsky (1964a, 1965, 1968); and Chomsky and Halle (1968). Chomsky
(1966b) is an article in which Chomsky repeats notions already
set forth elsewhere.

3.   For instance, Bolinger (1960b); Hill (1962b,1966); Austin
(1967); Lamb (1967); Chafe (1968).

4.   For instance, Uhlenbeck (1963, 1967); Winter (1965);
Grunig (1967); Herdan (1967); and my over-all survey in Hall
(1969b).

5.   There is no book published in Europe that gives a satisfactory picture of the development of linguistics in America from
1920 to 1960. The discussions in Leroy (1963) and M. Ivić (1965)
are quite inexact. G. Lepscky (1966:95-116) has at least read
Sapir and Bloomfield, but his understanding of the theories of the
different groups of "post-Bloomfieldians" leaves considerable to be
desired; cf. my review of Lepscky (1966) in Hall (1967).

6.   Cf. Hockett (1948).

7.   Until recently, Bloomfield (1933a) was available only in
English. A recent translation by Alberto Escobar (*Lenguaje*, Lima:
Universidad Nacional Mayor de San Marcos, 1964) gives the complete

text and adds a very useful supplementary bibliography.   [An Italian translation finally appeared in 1974, by Francesco Antinucci
and G. R. Cardona (Milano: Il Saggiatore; La Cultura, Biblioteca di
Linguistica, no. 3.]
    For details of the activities and publications of Sapir and
Bloomfield, cf. Hall (1950b).
    8. On this point, Sapir and Bloomfield were in complete agree-
ment; cf. Sapir (1931).
    9. We must insist on this point, because — under the influ-
ence of the inaccurate picture (virtually a caricature) given by
various historians of twentieth-century linguistics — it is widely
and falsely believed that Bloomfield was devoid of broader views
and even of personal feelings.
    10. Among the various groups engaged in such activities, the
most outstanding is the Summer Institute of Linguistics (founded
in 1925 by William Cameron Townsend), which, in close alliance
with the Wycliffe Bible Translators, has produced, in the past
three decades, almost four fifths of what has been published on
American Indian languages (cf. their bibliographies, published
from time to time, first at Glendale and later at Santa Ana, California [and most recently (1985) at Dallas, Texas].
    11. Cf. his observations in Bloomfield (1946), and those of
Fries (1961). Note the quotation marks around the word "school"
in Fries's title.
    12. This notion arose because the European war-time refugees
of the 1940's knew no American linguists except those centred on
New York and Yale University (in New Haven, only 75 miles from New
York), and, seeing the latter group's admiration for Bloomfield,
considered that they must form a "school". Furthermore, the position of Bernard Bloch as editor of *Language* was misinterpreted
as indicative of a dominance which he did not enjoy. In the first
edition of Kukenheim (1962), its author spoke (113) of this imaginary "Yale school"; in the second edition (1966:160, 175), he recognized its fictitious nature.
    13. Cf. my discussion in the first chapter of Hall (1968a).
    14. In those years, however, the gap and hostility between the
generations was perhaps the lowest that it has ever been in the
social sciences and the humanities. Among the most enthusiastic
members of our "group C" were George M. Bolling (1871-1963), Hans
Kurath (b. 1891), and Edgar H. Sturtevant (1876-1957). Bloomfield
was right when, describing the intellectual atmosphere of those
days, he said (1946:2) "Nowadays the older worker in linguistics
often learns from the younger, and has the supreme professional
satisfaction of knowing that the next generation is going forward
from the frontiers of what is known today".
    15. For this reason, G. Devoto (1964) was quite wrong in re-
ferring to a supposed "grigio conformismo" in American linguistics.
[This term would have applied much better to the state of affairs
in the 1960's and later, under the TGG mafia. — RAHjr, 1985.]
    16. In his 1914 book, Bloomfield had followed Wilhelm Wundt's
"Völkerpsychologie"; but later, after passing through a stage in
which he was influenced by the objectivist psychology of A. P.

Weiss (not, as is often asserted, the naïve variety of "behaviorism" expounded by J. B. Watson in his popularizing writings), he
came to the conclusion that the linguist should remain aloof from
any specific variety of psychology, and especially from any in
which the existence of permanently unobservable elements was postulated. On this point, the student should always read Bloomfield?s own writings; such accounts as that given by Schlauch
(1946) are quite untrustworthy.

17. The myth that Bloomfield denied the importance and even
the existence of meaning is still wide-spread, despite the acute
observations of Fries (1954). For recent exemplifications of this
misunderstanding, cf. the remarks of W. Bahner (in his translation
of Iordan [1961]), who speaks of this presumed superficiality of
Bloomfield's out-look (462), concluding with the Sybilline remark
that Bloomfield was "nicht in der Lage, das Phänomen Sprache in
seinem Wesen zu erfassen". Cf. also the observations of Meid
(1966). But see also Esper (1968), for a refutation of these
slanders.

18. These terms were invented, as far as I know, by Hockett
(1954).

19. As I pointed out in Hall (1965).

20. Exemplified in Lounsbury (1953), a thesis written under
Bloch's direction; cf. my review thereof (Hall [1954]).

21. Especially the following (listed here in chronological order): Bloch and Trager (1942); Z. S. Harris (1951); Trager and
Smith (1951); Hockett (1955, 1958).

22. Cf. Pike (1943, 1947a, 1948, 1954 [1967^2]), and Nida
(1946, 1951). Cf. also Elson and Pickett (1962).

23. Cf. Nida (1947).

24. Pike (1947b, 1954).

25. Fries and Pike (1949).

26. As an example, I shall describe my own experience in this
respect. My first teacher in linguistics was Hoijer, with Sapir
(1921) as text. When Bloomfield (1933a) appeared, I read and re-
read it attentively, but it took several years before I realized
that his opposition to psychologizing did not constitute a denial
of an essential part of human experience. For that matter, I have
never been convinced of certain of Bloomfield's notions, e.g. that
society is an organism (with language performing a function parallel to that of the nervous system in a living body), or his analysis of English vowels.

27. It has repeatedly been remarked that Chomsky is in the habit of badly misrepresenting and distorting the views of those who
disagree with him; cf. the observations of Lamb (1967:414-415).
Chomsky's disciples have carried this fault of his to an extreme,
as did Katz (1964), whose tone was rightly termed "scurrilous" by
Hockett (1965), in an article generally favorable to Chomsky.

28. Garvin (1963), reviewing Jakobson (ed.) (1961).

29. Cf. the acute observations of Longacre (1964:13-14).

30. Cf. Koutsoudas (1963), and the added remarks of C. F.
Voegelin and others at the end of this article.

31. Cf. Halle (1962) and Stockwell (1960).

32. Saltarelli (1970); cf. Hall (1972c).

33. Chomsky (1966a) interprets the difference between Vaugelas
and the Port-Royal grammar as if it were an anticipation of that
between the hated "post-Bloomfieldians" (mere classifiers, superficial taxonomists) and himself. Protests have already been made
against Chomsky's many inaccuracies in this book (one of the few
in which he has condescended to pay attention to observable facts),
as pointed out in Hall (1970). The defects of this opuscule of
Chomsky's are all the more evident when it is compared with the
solid and highly meritorious study by Donzé (1967), which appeared
at almost the same time but was overshadowed, for the general public, by Chomsky's meretricious pot-boiler.

34. In the famous Introduction to Boas (ed.) (1911).

35. Cf. the excellent material in Greenberg (ed.) (1963), con-
taining papers presented at a meeting held in 1961.

36. Beginning with Chomsky (1957a). We must note that the
term "correctness" refers, in this context, not to obedience to
the prescriptions of some academy or other "authority", but to
the simplicity and elegance of a solution, as in a mathematical
problem.

37. Cf. Joos (1961).

38. Halle (1962:54).

39. Cf. the intelligent observations of Hill (1961).

40. Cf. the declaration of Postal (1964:262) that "It is evident that actual verbal performances contain an enormous number of
utterances which do not in the strict sense represent any sentences at all" [!].

41. I have attempted to show (Hall [1963]) the harm done to
linguistics, especially in the Romance field, by "idealism".

42. Cf. Hall (1972a).

43. For instance, M. Bierwisch (1966:16) speaks of Chomsky's
"mathematicization" as "a break-through of the first importance in
linguistic science and the only result of importance the mathematical branch of linguistics has had so far". Hockett, also, at a
certain point in the development of his thought (1965:196 ff.),
expressed a like opinion.

44. Cf. the programmatic article of Katz and Fodor (1963).

45. As rightly observed by Garvin (1963).

46. I have already remarked elsewhere (Hall [1968b]) that
Bloomfield himself, if he had not died prematurely, would undoubtedly have contributed greatly to the criticism of these excesses,
as he had already begun to do in Bloomfield (1945).

47. In Fries (1925) and elsewhere, especially in his two very
important books on English grammar (Fries [1940, 1951]). Cf. also
the very severe criticisms of traditional grammar in Bloomfield
(1933a:496 ff.) and others, e.g. Hall (1950a).

48. Cf. the defense of certain traditional views — e.g. the
rule for the use of the nominative of a pronoun after *than* in constructions like *he is richer than I*, instead of *than me* (which is,
however, far more frequent in every-day use) — in Roberts
(1966: p. T-11); or Hathaway (1967), which is the best demonstration of the essentially reactionary nature of transformational

grammar once it is stripped of its pseudo-mathematical trappings.

49. Such considerations have not deterred Chomsky from introducing political considerations into his books on linguistics as
well, especially *Cartesian Linguistics* (Chomsky [1966a: 91-93,
110-111]).

50. Chomsky (1957b).

51. Cf. Hockett (1966), a long article also issued as a separate monograph.

52. Hockett (1965:196-200).

53. Characteristic of Hockett's scientific attitude and behavior is the fact that he sent two successive versions of this formulation to Chomsky for the latter's criticisms and corrections,
so as to give the most accurate presentation possible of Chomsky's position.

54. Expounded in David (1958).

55. In the Introduction to Boas (ed.) (1911).

56. This is not the only instance that Hockett could have
cited of Chomsky's unscrupulous way of using ambiguous terminology,
or of choosing terms which have emotional over-tones, as in his
choice of the expression "surface" and "deep" for structure. The
naïve reader has learned from childhood to regard what is on the
surface as less valuable or important than what is "deep" and
difficult of access. More exact and objective terms would have
been "derived" and "starting-point", with regard to structure.

57. For the semantic passage of words meaning 'to know > to
be in the habit of', cf. Lida de Malkiel (1948/49).

58. The classic example of this phenomenon is when a child
says *I'm hungry* when it is in reality not hungry at all, but simply wants to get out of going to bed, as pointed out by Bloomfield
(1933a:142). The only way to determine the meaning of any utterance or its elements, in a given context, is to examine the situation and to determine with which of its aspects the linguistic
phenomena are correlated.

59. One of the favorite assertions of Chomsky's followers is
that their analyses are so well founded in theory that they cannot
be overturned by concrete data — an open confession of the antiscientific character of their work.

60. Protests against this revival of the notion of innate i-
deas have not been lacking, e.g. Putnam (1967).

61. That is, that phonetic change would be regular if there
were no intervening disturbing factors. For a defense of this
scientific assumption — which, as Otto Jespersen remarked, many
deny in theory but none neglect in practice — cf. Hall (1957).

62. Floods of ink have been spilled on the problem of lying,
mostly from the philosophical and logical point of view, with little attention to its linguistic aspects; cf. Weinrich (1966). From
the linguistic angle, two factors permit people to lie: negation
and displaced speech, i.e. the possibility of speaking of something when it is not present in the immediate context of speech.

63. E.g. Francescato (1958).

64. As I remarked in Hall (1968b).

65. Cf. Hall (1968a:316, note 1; 1968c).

SOME CRITIQUES OF CHOMSKYAN THEORY*

(Neuphilologische Mitteilungen 78.86-95 [1977])

Since 1957, an approach to the description of language known as
transformational-generative grammar (TGG) has been set forth in the
writings of A. N. Chomsky (especially 1957a, 1964a, 1964b, 1966b,
1967b, 1968; for a complete bibliography to 1975, cf. Karrer and
Palascak [1976]), and spread by his followers. By the mid-1970's,
the TGG approach and the theoretical approach underlying it had
become a dominant orthodoxy in North American circles (cf. A. Makkai [1974] — but also McCawley [1975]) and widely influential
elsewhere (cf., for instance, Ruwet [1967]; Bierwisch [1971] — but
also Maher's review [1974]; and many others). If not a "paradigm"
in the narrow sense originally proposed by Kuhn (1961; cf. Anttila
[1974]), the TGG approach has been at least a "cynosure" (the term
suggested by Hymes [ed.] [1974:20-23]) for the past two decades.
It has been so prestigious as to induce theorists in other fields
to adopt Chomskyan concepts and terminology, as in the (quite unsuccessful) effort of Bernstein (1976) to discover the "deep structure" of music. From the out-set, the theories of Chomsky and his
followers have been subjected to critical examination, which has,
however, not received the attention it deserves. It is my intent
here to discuss the major critiques that have been made of Chomsky's view of language and the analysis thereof, with regard to
linguistic structure; the activities of humans in using language;
its "innateness"; the types of analysis practised by Chomsky and
his disciples; the relation of linguistics to other disciplines;
and his view of the history of the field.

The most serious objections to Chomsky's view of linguistic
structure are based on the fact that he treats language as if it
were a well-defined system, closed, rigid, and static (as shown
by Hockett [1968:40, 56-59]. As a result, the Chomskyan model of
language neglects the openness of linguistic structures — the
fact that they are by no means wholly neat, logical, coherent systems. If language were indeed as Chomsky views it, there would be
no possibility of its changing in the course of time. Yet, ever
since Dante observed (De vulgari Eloquentia 1.ix.6):

    omnis loquela [...] nec durabilis nec continua esse

---

* I have deliberately omitted all references to my own critiques
of the Chomskyan approach.

potest; sed sicut alia quae nostra sunt, puta
mores et habitus, per locorum temporumque dis-
tantias variari oportet [...]

'No language can be lasting or continuous; but, like other things
of ours, such as customs and habits, it has to vary over distances
of time and space", mutability has been known to be a prime characteristic of language. At the centre of every linguistic system
there is indeed a core of relatively consistent patterns. Even
these, however, are subject to what Hockett (1968:61) has termed
"rubbery constraints"; and at its edges there are always loose
ends on all levels of language.

One of the main factors contributing to the illusion that language is rigid and wholly stable has been the almost exclusively
written nature of the materials on which Chomsky and his followers
have based their analyses. Hence many aspects of linguistic communication have been neglected or their effects have been pushed into
grammar when they actually belong in pronunciation, especially intonation (cf. Pap [1976:5]). Intonation has typically been treated
by TGG theorists (e.g. Stockwell [1960]) as completely secondary to
and determined by grammar, whereas it is in actuality the first aspect of linguistic structure learned by the child (cf. von Raffler
- Engel [1966, 1972]). It is the basis on which all the rest of
meaningful linguistic communication is built up, not a mere tonal
respesentation of grammatical concepts. For instance, Bolinger
(1967) has demonstrated conclusively that English imperatives are
distinguished from other types of sentence by their intonation, not
by any kind of transformation.

Is language an individual or a social activity? It is of
course both, in that it has its place of existence exclusively in
individuals, but it is used for social purposes, in each individual's talking to others or to him- or herself. The Chomskyan insistence on a generative approach has led, however, to a very one-sided bias, with exclusive attention to the rôle of the speaker. Chomsky's repeated assertions that he is dealing with an "ideal speaker-listener" do not carry conviction, in view of his neglect of the
importance of a speaker's reaction to and interpretation of what he
or she hears (cf. Hockett [1961]). Faust (1970:46) rightly observed "In effect, Chomsky's ideal speaker-listener is not in a
speech-community at all. He is a lone individual, completely surrounded by speech-mirrors".

Human language is of course meaningful, and communication among
humans is its prime function, as recognized in almost all basic discussions of language, such as Sapir (1921:13-17, 38-42), Bloomfield
(1933a:139-157), Hockett (1958:139-144, 570-585), etc. As pointed
out by Hockett (1968:67-75; cf. also Grunig [1966:55-71]), Chomsky
at first continued the error of his mentor Z. S. Harris (e.g.
[1951:186-195, 363) of regarding grammar as "a self-contained study
independent of semantics" (Chomsky 1957a:106) and of regarding mean-

ing as something super-added after the "generation" of structural
combinations. But grammar, although it may be autonomous, cannot
be independent of meaning, as many have observed, from Reichling
(1961:3-5) to Gray (1974) and Bolinger (1976). Nor can one have
the abstract, mathematical precision of form and at the same time
account for all the workaday semantic contingencies, as Reichling
put it. In his later discussions (1965 and after), Chomsky has had
to recognize the existence and relevance of meaning (cf. Saint-Jacques [1967:28-29]), but has pushed it into an inaccessible and un-
provable "deep structure". As applied to English, Chomskyan "deep
structure" is only the stripped-down syntactic essential of a major clause, with the elements SUBJECT and PREDICATE taken over uncritically from our unsatisfactory traditional grammar (as pointed
out by Uhlenbeck [1975:108-111]). In the case of non-English languages, their "deep structure" usually turns out, curiously enough,
to be simply the English equivalent of their constructions (cf.,
for example, Noss [1972] for Thai), which are thus squeezed into
the Procrustean bed of English grammar in exactly the same way that
earlier descriptions forced non-Latin languages into the Latin
mould (cf. Collinder [1970]; Théban and Théban [1971/72]; Steiner
[1975:106]). Hence Chomsky has (as observed by Uhlenbeck [1975:
30-31, 55-56, 89-101]) minimized the semantic aspect of language
and maximized its syntactic aspect, with resultant imbalance and
distortion.

That the "surface structures" of languages differ from each o-
ther, every-one knows. But Chomsky has consistently subordinated
the study of "surface" phenomena to that of "deep structure",
claiming that the latter is the only basis on which linguistic theory can accomplish what he (1965:15) has described as its main
task, "to develop an account of linguistic universals" and a "general grammar" based thereon. Given the inaccessible nature of "deep
structure", these universals can never be arrived at by mere comparison of data from various languages and by cross-language generalizations (as attempted, say, in Greenberg [ed.] [1963]). The task
can be accomplished only by aprioristic speculation, of the type
exemplified in Bach and Harms (ed.) (1967). As Hockett (1968:66)
has said, any search for such a "general grammar" is no more than
a snipe-hunt. The same point is made by Steiner (1975:98-108).
As the latter has said (1975:95), "each level of proposed universality has been found to be contingent or subverted by anomalies.
[...] Instead of being rigorous and exhaustive, the description of
'universal linguistic traits' has often proved to be no more than
an open-ended catalogue".

The distinction between "deep" and "surface" structure is correlated with a two-way opposition between "competence" and "performance". These two concepts are obviously similar to the Saussurean pair of *langue* and *parole*, not in their meaning of collective versus individual usage, but as they refer to the total potential of a speaker's language-activity as opposed to its partial
manifestations on single occasions. Both the Chomskyan and the

Saussurean pairs suffer from the inevitable defect of binary oppositions, in that they exclude third possibilities. Chomsky has
failed to distinguish between innate, species-specific CAPACITY to
learn and use linguistic systems, on the one-hand, and the KNOW-HOW
which each individual acquires as he grows up in a given speech-
community and learns its particular language on the other. But
this distinction is very old, and was effectively formulated by
Dante in the well-known passage of *Paradiso* 26.130-132:

> Opera naturale è ch'uom favella;
> Ma così o così, Natura lascia
> Poi fare a voi, secondo che v'abbella

'It is an effect of the way that he is born that man speaks; but in
this way or that, Nature leaves it up to you, as best pleases you'.
By merging the speaker's know-how with his (unquestionably genetically determined) capacity to learn a language, Chomsky has constructed an abstract, by-definition-perfect "competence" which
corresponds to nothing observable or deducible from observed facts
and is useless for the description of any language, as has been
remarked by many critics, such as Hockett (1968:77), Twaddell
(1973:324-325), Esper (1973:166-167), Derwing (1973:259-266), Uhlenbeck (1975:40-56, 102-108), Robinson (1975:57-69), Hammarström
(1976:vi-vii, 64 [fn. 83], 65 [fn. 86]), Kates (1976).

By neglecting the individual's rôle as hearer, Chomsky has se-
verely limited the possibilities of accounting for the ontogenesis
of each dialect. If one denies, as Chomsky has consistently done
(1959 and many other places) that a speaker forms his or her idiolect through imitation of other speakers, one manoeuvers oneself
into a position where, in theorizing, one has to rely only on what
the speaker brings to his own linguistic development. Chomsky has
tried to get out of this corner into which he has painted himself,
by hypothesizing an innate "Language-Acquisition-Device" or
"L.A.D." (1966b:10, and many later writings); cf. also Derwing
(1973:50-53). For the existence of such a special device — as
distinct from the normal processes of human learning — there is no
evidence. As Putnam (1967:20) has remarked, Chomsky's argument in
favor of innateness reduces to saying "Wow! How complicated a
skill every normal adult learns. What else could it be but innate?". (Cf. also Saint-Jacques [1967:37-40], Twaddell [1973:320-
323], Uhlenbeck [1975:55-56], and Robinson [1975:69-73].)

As a matter of fact, linguistic structure is not all that complicated, and Stemmer (1973) has demonstrated that there is no need,
from an abstract theoretical point of view, to consider human language-learning as in any way different from the other learning-ac-
tivities of people or animals. From recent discussions (e.g. Peng
[1975]; Hebb, Lambert and Tucker [1971]), it is evident that, with
a broader approach and taking perceptual learning and S-S reactions
into account, it is not necessary to treat heredity and environment
as mutually exclusive factors in the learning of language or any-

thing else. The assumption of a special "L.A.D." is also contra-
dicted by direct observation of the way children learn their first
language (cf. von Raffler - Engel [1970, 1974]).

The technique of TGG description consists essentially in establishing a series of rules — instructions to a human or to a ma-
chine — by whose application a given combination of elements will
be replaced by another combination, going only in one direction.
There is an element of apriorism inherent in such a procedure, in
that it requires an absolutely definite set of data to start with,
and, at each point of the procedure, no indeterminacy can be admitted. Data gathered from the observation of real people's real
language-activity, however, inevitably show all kinds of indeterminacy. Ill-definedness is an essential characteristic of linguistic systems (cf. Hockett [1968:59-69]). But in TGG work, anything indeterminate must be excluded *a priori* (cf. Reichling
[1961:16-17]). Chomsky has, from the very beginning, shown far
greater concern for the "correctness" of rule-concoction than for
the completeness or even the accuracy of the data to be analysed
(cf. Hockett [1968:76]) — whence his well-known contempt for "dis-
covery-procedures" and the need for Longacre (1964).

There is also an element of circularity in the choice of only
"well-formed" sentences to be studied. As Noss (1972:10) has put
it, "well-formed sentences are those sentences which are generated
by the strict application of rules derived from inspection of well-
formed sentences". This is the same circularity which we find in
traditional prescriptive grammar, and for a good reason. TGG analysis makes essentially the same kind of statement in terms of prescriptive rules, but couched in very concise, quasi-mathematical
formulae. As Uhlenbeck (1975:7-8) has observed,

> The syntactic analysis which Chomsky employs is of a
> highly traditional type. In fact it is the traditional
> way of parsing as is done practically everywhere in
> school. This system of parsing rests on the wrong as-
> sumption to which may generations of students of syntax
> have clung tenaciously, that an analysis of a sentence
> is a kind of gradual division of its content.

Without a criterion of well-formedness (grammaticality, correctness — they all amount to the same thing), neither traditional
grammar nor TGG can function. The discrepancy between the requirement of grammaticality and the actual facts of language was
observed quite early on, by Hill (1961), and has been pointed out
again by Grunig (1966:62-64) and Hawkey (1970).

Unnatural collations of elements have furnished a large part of
the rater scanty and scattered data on which much of Chomsky's and
his followers' extensive theorizing has been based (cf. Saint
Jacques [1967:35-36]). Such unlikely phrases as *flying planes can
be dangerous* or *the shooting of the hunters* have attracted some

well-deserved ridicule (e.g. Noss [1972]). It has been remarked
(e.g. by Uhlenbeck [1975:27]) that these few phrases are normally
cited, in Chomskyan discussions, in an anecdotal fashion, over and
over again, by themselves and out of context. Many expressions or
sentences which are branded "ambiguous" or "ungrammatical", in
their written form, are perfectly clear and normal when they occur
with the appropriate intonation and in an appropriate context.
Thus (one instance out of many), *John's book in the woods*, which
Chomsky (1970:197) has said "we cannot form", is perfectly possible if we are contrasting two books, one of which John keeps at
home and the other in the woods (cf. Noss [1972:9]). For other
examples of Chomsky's misapprehensions with regard to what we can
and cannot say, cf. Robinson (1975:141-144]).

Chomskyan discussion of language is almost wholly framed in
terms reflecting concern with written representations and formulae. Pap (1976:5) has phrased this objection well:

> Probably because transformational-generative theory
> has grown up largely in a milieu (such as M.I.T.) do-
> minated by mathematics, symbolic logic, and engineering,
> by blackboard formulas and graphs, this school not only
> loves symbolic notations and diagrams, but it also likes
> to speak of "switching" elements from right to left, from
> left to right, up or down. In this and other ways (for
> instance in the frequent disregard of prosodic features
> in analyzing sentences, TG authors show an unhealthy
> tendency to talk about language as if it were primarily
> written, rather than spoken.

As Pap further observes, the Chomskyan use of LEFT and RIGHT, to
refer to the temporal sequence of linguistic elements, is naïvely
ethnocentric, deriving from Western alphabetic writing-habits.
TGG has been almost exclusive concerned with what Esper (1968:222,
225) has termed "paper-and-pencil manipulations" and has neglected
real-life language-behavior, especially as this latter involves
the passage of time in speaking.

The same characteristics we have been discussing in connection
with the Chomskyan view of language in general — rigidity, the
assumption of an undemonstrable "deep structure" (named, for phonological purposes, "underlying representation"), abstract "competence", artificial well-definedness, and derivation from written
from written representation — reappear in "generative phonology",
baginning with Halle (1962). This approach was exposed as inadequate by Householder (1965, 1966), and was rightly characterized
by Hockett (1968:4) as "bankrupt". The appearance of Chomsky and
Halle (1968) confirmed Hockett's characterization, a view upheld
by later critics, e.g. Hammarström (1971, 1973, 1976), Maher
(1973, 1976), Lamb and Vanderslice (1975), and Christie (1976).

Almost from its inception, ancient and modern Western interest in language and its analysis have been tied in with philosophy and logic (cf. Robins [1951, 1967]). In the nineteenth century, psychology, in its new-found independence from philosophy, was also extensively concerned with linguistic matters, though often on a basis of introspection and arm-chair philosophizing (cf. Esper [1968:152-153]). Littérateurs and aestheticians also considered themselves competent to make pronouncements on linguistic theory, as did Croce (1902) and Vossler (1904, 1905). It has taken linguists nearly a century and a half to free their discipline from its ancillary status vis-à-vis these earlier-established fields, and to achieve the autonomy which most linguists have recognized as essential to its growth and development; cf., for instance, Bloomfield (1925), Sapir (1929), and so forth, down to Hockett (1977). Chomsky, however, has robbed linguistics of its hard-won independence, by handing it back as a hand-maiden to philosophy, logic, and psychology (and out-worn varieties of these fields, at that). In so doing, he has neglected the much closer relation of linguistics to cultural anthropology (cf. Hockett [1968:79-80]) and to the humanities (cf. Robinson [1975:174-196]). Linguistics is, as a result, greatly in need of re-humanizing (Yngve [1974]).

In presenting his theories, which are so largely opposed to the discoveries of pre-1957 linguistics, Chomsky has adopted what Voegelin and Voegelin (1963) have termed the "eclipsing stance", denigrating much (if not most) of what was accomplished in the previous century. His presentation of both recent and earlier work has given his readers a badly distorted picture. What Lamb (1967) says of Chomsky (1965) is a good description of Chomskyan polemic technique in general:

> A parade of specious arguments, it makes use of the
> shifting meaning, a device which the author has devel-
> oped to a high degree of refinement. The essence of
> this device is the sliding of terms from one meaning
> to another. Supplemented by the complementary strategy
> of moving meanings from one term to another, the de-
> vice is used in attacks upon real or imaginary oppon-
> ents in mock battles set up for the occasion.

Chomsky's tendency to misrepresent others' views has become notorious; cf., for example, Wiest (1967), Hockett (1968:63-64 Faust (1970:44-45), Twaddell (1973), Aarsleff (1974:115-121). In some instances, his criticisms have been so wide of the mark that they have simply not dealt with the matter in hand, as in his 1959 review of Skinner (1957). This review, in particular, has been repeatedly anthologized and its allegations have been widely but uncritically accepted as valid. MacCorquodale's demonstration (1969) of the unfounded nature of Chomsky's aspersions on Skinner has remained virtually unknown to linguists (cf. also Esper [1973:196, fn. 60]).

The relation of Chomsky's theories to those of earlier periods

— essentially the "general grammar" movement of the seventeenth and eighteenth centuries, beginning with the Port-Royal grammar of 1660 — has likewise been badly misrepresented, particularly by Chomsky (1966a), in his search for antecedents for his theories. The non-existence of "Cartesian linguistics" and Chomsky's misunderstanding of the relationship between the Port-Royal grammar and Vaugelas, have been amply demonstrated by several scholars, e.g. Aarsleff (1970, 1971, 1974), Dostert (1972), Joly (1972) and Percival (1972, 1976). Unfortunately, the publicity and (completely unjustified) prestige accorded Chomsky's misrepresentation has been so great as to overshadow the serious, solid, and well-founded study of Port-Royal by Donzé (1967). As a result of Chomsky's over-emphasis on seventeenth-century rationalism, the very real contributions of sixteenth-century scholarship have been neglected (cf. Izzo [1976a, 1976b]).

Not all the critiques that have been made of Chomsky's theories are themselves immune to criticism. Robinson (1975) is perhaps the worst offender. He is excellent in all his animadversions, which he presents with trenchant observations and pungent wit. He clearly knows too little, however, of pre-Chomskyan linguistics to offer any concrete alternatives, except a return to the study of literature and the theories of Croce (!). The late Gustav Herdan (1967, 1968) presented his objections clearly and concisely, but was so petulant and abrasive in his rhetoric that the editors of the Zeitschrift für Phonetik inserted an apologetic foot-note. The only place to refute Chomskyan theories is on their own ground of abstraction; but by so doing, Hockett (1968) laid himself open to the unjustified charge of G. Lakoff (1969) that he was neglecting facts. Similarly, Stemmer (1973) presents extensive theoretical arguments, but with surprisingly few concrete examples. The merits of these critiques greatly outweigh any faults they may have, but they have been largely neglected. There are at least four reasons for this neglect:

(1) Many of them have been published in out-of-the-way places [because the normal channels of communication in North America were closed to them — RAHjr, 1985];

(2) Chomskyan theorists are, by and large, singularly obtuse to criticism;

(3) The field has been entered by a whole generation of students who "are led to the false impression that all linguists before Chomsky (except, of course, Humboldt, Sapir, and a few other candidates for canonization) were hopelessly misguided bumblers, from whose clutches Chomsky has heroically rescued the field of linguistics" (Lamb [1967:414]);

(4) Irrelevant political considerations have been introduced, as when Bracken (1972:6) condemned opposition to Chomsky's views by calling it "a counter-revolutionary subordination of scholarship".

Nevertheless, taken together, the criticisms we have just
briefly discussed constitute a devastating refutation of all aspects of Chomskyan theory. His view of language itself and the
study thereof have been weighed in the balance and found wanting.
Of his contribution, what is likely to survive? — a few signs, such
as the very useful ← and → for synchronic replacement, as opposed
to diachronic change indicated by < and >, and a few techniques
for compressing the formulation of linguistic phenomena into space-
saving quasi-algebraic notation. Transformations are indeed a
helpful addition to the study of syntactic and derivational relations, but in their Harrisian, not their Chomskyan form (cf.
Twaddell [1972]). The generative approach, with its inherent narrowness imposed by its unidirectional nature, is insufficient for
the adequate description of syntax or other aspects of linguistic
structure such as morphology (cf. Dik [1967]). "Deep structure"
simply does not exist; it is an arbitrary invention, an unnecessary
obstruction to syntactic analysis, and should be excised by Occam's
razor (cf. Coseriu [1969]; Collinder [1970]; Danielsen [1971,
1972]; Rommetveit [1972]). Even the earlier avatar of "deep structure," syntactic "kernels", cannot always be postulated to account
for all syntactic phenomena (Winter [1965]). For the rest, the
sooner we return to the moderation advocated by Garvin (1970), the
better.

REVIEW OF HAGÈGE, *LA GRAMMAIRE GÉNÉRATIVE*

(Forum Linguisticum 2.75-79 [1977])

Criticisms of the transformational-generative (TG) approach to the description of language have been increasing in number and intensity in recent years (cf. Hall [1977]). Most of the critiques have been in the shape of articles, many of them published in relatively out-of-the-way journals. Of the major book-length discussions, Hockett (1968) deals primarily with the abstract theoretical foundations of Chomskyan doctrines. Uhlenbeck (1975) is a reprint of previously published articles. Robinson (1975) presents a series of excellent negative animadversions, but with insufficient knowledge of non-TG linguistics to offer any constructive alternatives. There was clearly need for a thorough, full-sized analysis of Chomskyan theory and its shortcomings, by a linguist with knowledge of a number of languages, especially non-English and non-Indo-European. Hagège has worked extensively on African, Asian and American Indian languages, and has a good grasp of the principles of linguistic analysis, primarily but not exclusively of the Martinetian type. His book is, therefore, of just the kind that was needed.

In his first chapter, 'Le cadre intellectuel et social' (11-51), H gives a perceptive sketch of the background out of which the TG movement grew and discusses its relation to other varieties of linguistics. He rightly ascribes (20-25) the rapid success and spread of TG doctrines to, not only the inevitable reaction against 'le formalisme distributionaliste' (21) and the arrogance of TG partisans (25-27), but also their appeal to those who were made insecure by a structuralist approach. Such people, of whom there were many, were reassured by Chomsky's return to traditional grammatical categories, charmed by his pseudo-mathematical elegance, enthused by his oversimplified radical chic (with a veneer of philosophy), and hypnotized by his techniques of aggressive but deceptive argumentation (cf. Lamb [1967:414]). In his 'Profil du monde générativiste' (25-51), H emphasizes the TG school's dogmatism, their 'eclipsing stance' and their 'selective ignorance', coupled with misrepresentation and attempted absorption of preceding generations and epochs. A particularly felicitous term is *ravaudage* or 'patching-up', which, as H points out (39-41), TG doctrines have to undergo as they are constantly revised to correct their original oversimplified formulation. He also emphasizes (49-51), as many other critics have done, the continual reliance of TG theorists on English for their examples, and their use of it as a Procrustean bed into which all other languages are forced (much, we may add, to the ego-satisfaction of Anglophones).

Chapter II, 'Linguistique et science dans la vision générative'
(52-95), is a critical examination of the TG approach to scientific
method, with emphasis on the vacillations and contradictions inherent in Chomskyan attitudes towards empirical data. That IG theories neglect facts in favor of aprioristic doctrine, considering
mere data 'uninteresting' unless they confirm theory (Schreiber
[1974]) is well known. One irreparable disaster that is lilely to
result from this desire to replace investigation by theorizing is
that, as H emphasizes (56-61), the disapprearance of the already
vanishing languages of 'primitive' peoples, which are of such
great value for our knowledge of the possible range of linguistic
phenomena. In TG theory, unvalidated suppositions easily become
flat assertions concerning unobserved and unobservable entities,
such as the notorious Language-Acquisition-Device (62-64). Chomskyan generativism is essentially Platonic and idealistic in its
nature (64-68), and it is this antiscientific bias that has conditioned the TG dogmas concerning competence and performance (72-78),
language-learning (79-84), and universals (84-96). These last-
mentioned are essential to the postulation of innate deep structures and the L.A.D.; yet those proposed *a priori* by Chomsky, Halle
and others have at best a limited application as soon as we take
attested data from real languages into account.

The central chapter of the book is the third, 'Les opérations
et les niveaux' (97-172), a severe criticism of Chomskyan procedure
with respect to the passage from deep to surface structure and its
relation to meaning and the lexicon (97-145) and the problem of
phonemics vis-à-vis phonetics and morphophonemics (146-172). Here,
as elsewhere, Chomskyan terminology and concepts have been fluctu-
ating and variable (97-101), and are much closer to earlier 'taxonomic' models than is normally admitted (101-107). What is the exact place of deep structure and its relation to the surface, i.e.
the actual utterance, on the one hand, and to meaning on the other?
TG doctrines are very confused on this point, and inconsistent even
with regard to English, to say nothing of other languages (107-115).
Nor do transformations by any means always correspond to the actual
process of speaking (cf. also Pulgram [1967?83]). They are often
arbitrary and *ad hoc*, with added or subtracted elements devoid of
real existence, leading on occasion to *un vrai délire effaceur*
'deletion gone hog-wild' (115-121). Neither Chomskyan lexicalism
nor generative semantics, with its reliance on formalistic logic
(which is basically irrelevant to the study of real language) are
adequate to account for the total use of language in all possible
contexts (121-132). The source of the confusion lies, as H rightly
observes (132-157), in Chomsky's and his successors' false equa-
tion between synonymy and paraphrase on the one hand, and deep
structure on the other, because 'sense' has been reduced to 'desig-
nation'. As H says (135): 'La frontière entre la langue et le réel
est brouillée, et on donne l'*équivalence designationnelle* pour une
synonymie linguistique' [italics his]. Ambiguity, an essential
and necessary characteristic of human language (cf. also Noss
[1972]) is, in TG analysis, unrealistically banished from deep

structure, arbitrarily defined as purely logical (137-142). It is probable that, as the formulation of deep-to-surface relations becomes more complicated and implies more specific consequences, the distance between 'deep' and 'surface' will become proportionately less. Meanwhile, generative linguistics has gotten us no forrader in understanding the nature of meaning (145).

The relation of phonology to morphosyntax, and the extension of generative analysis to phonological structure, has been one of the least satisfactory aspects of TG theory. After a brief history (147-153) of the generativists' 'crusade' against the phoneme — an attack based largely on misunderstandings and misrepresentations, especially of Bloch's phonemics — H discusses 'the morphophonemic option' (153-163) and the generativists' reliance on binary oppositions (164-169). Here, as elsewhere, H finds that 'ce sont encore des exigences formelles de présentation qui ordonnent un édifice appliqué à l'objet réel qu'est le phonétisme d'un langage (163) — in other words, the desired picture determines in advance the characteristics chosen to be portrayed. The list of possible binary oppositions is not *a priori* limited to a finite number (165). In many instances, especially tonal languages, the contrasts are not reducible to oppositions between discrete elements (168-169). The phoneme, officially disavowed, will not stay banished, and has had to be re-incorporated into phonological theory (171).

Chapter IV discusses 'La démarche formelle et la rigueur théorique' (173-226), pointing out chiefly the inconsistences and internal contradictions that have characterized Chomskyan doctrines since their inception. Excessive 'rigor' in formulation leads to a basically mechanistic approach, despite Chomsky's insistence on 'creativity' (173-186), and the quest for simplicity as a primary goal renders theory inadequate to deal with reality (187-192). If the 'ideal speaker-listener' were really a listener as well as a speaker, there would be no need to exclude biuniqueness from the requirements for stating linguistic relationships (191-192). Formalization inevitably implies that the linguistic material must be restricted to what constitutes a norm (194-202). The new norm, that of an individual's usage, constitutes a restricted corpus of just the type against which Chomsky has inveighed (194-196). As many critics have observed, such a narrow norm-based corpus inevitably differs from one individual to another, and leads to endless debate over insoluble problems of grammaticality and acceptability. Language serves, not only for communication regarding facts and ideas, but also for 'phatic communion', emotional expression, and similar non-logical functions. It inevitably varies, not only from one individual to another, but also from one group to the next. The TG approach neglects all these variations, because their recognition would invalidate its normative, absolutistic basis (198-207). TG attempts to deal with historical change have been unsuccessful, because its static, normative model excludes, by its very nature, the possibility of phonetic change and of analogy, to say nothing

of humor, metaphor, and, in general, any non-literal use of language (207-226).

In a brief, aptly named section, 'Pour ne pas conclure" (227-
229), H emphasizes that the TG approach has largely failed to live
up to its promises, even in syntax and semantics, and has gotten
the study of individual languages and their diversity (which is an
essential part of general linguistics) bogged down while TG linguists go off on a wild-goose-chase after universals. TG theory
is at the same time too narrow to satisfy the 'maximalists' (those
who want linguistics to embrace all aspects of communication) and
too thinly spread for the 'minimalists' (those who, with Trager
[1963], maintain that 'linguistics is linguistics' and not, say,
poetics or semiotics). Like even the most determined opponents of
the TG approach, H considers that some of its procedures and for-
malizations will continue to be useful adjuncts to linguistics. A
brief, not wholly complete list of references (231-242) and an index of languages (243-244) conclude the book.

The greatest merit of H's book is that it brings together between two covers virtually all the objections that have been raised
to date against Chomskyan theory (and adds some more of H's own),
upholding them with concrete evidence, much of which reflects H's
knowledge of languages other than English and French. His style is
somewhat involved; often, a given sentence contains so much information that the reader wishes it had been broken down into two or
more sentences. (Leonard Bloomfield's concision combined with ut-
most clarity has unfortunately had few imitators.) Yet H's wealth
of observations and perceptions renders his book highly valuable.

A few scattered comments:

42: In addition to the TG practitioners' penchant for humorous
names for their rules, papers and meetings — in which H rightly
sees no harm — mention might have been made of the fondness shown
by some (not all) of them for obscenity and politically biased examples.

69: H cites Hockett's expression of surprise at the popularity
of Chomskyan doctrines in the U.S.S.R. — which, however, is not
hard to understand in view of their absolutism and universalism.

135: Like many others, H fails to understand the insistence of
Bloomfield (1933a:78) that 'the meanings of speech-forms could be
scientifically defined only if all branches of science, including
especially psychology and physiology, were close to perfection'.
Bloomfield's observation is valid from either a mentalistic or a
non-mentalistic point of view. The meaning of a linguistic form is
the correlation between it and its non-linguistic referent, and
this correlation exists only inside each speaker (whether we say
'in the speaker's mind' or 'in his brain and central nervous system' is irrelevant.) To analyse and describe this correlation —

including all the personal connotations involved, which are just as
much a part of meaning as denotation — we should have to have thorough information concerning, not only the referent of each form,
but also the total life-history and experiences of each speaker in
connection therewith. Of course we have not, and shall not have in
the foreseeable future, any such information; so we all, whether
mentalists or non-mentalists, have to 'makee do' with approximations.

149: H's observation 'l'enthousiasme des apprentis linguistes
mobilisés par le *war effort* et appliquant les méthodes des succes-
seurs de Bloomfield semble avoir causé un abus de l'étiquette' is
puzzling. The linguists who worked in the I[ntensive] L[anguage]
P[rogram] and other war-programs were not apprentices, but fully
competent scholars, who were for the most part the very 'successors
of Bloomfield' referred to. What 'abuses' is H referring to?

219: That the notion of the paradigm appeared 'mentalistic' to
Bloomfield is by no means true. Bloomfield (1933a:223-236, esp.
229-231, etc.) gives extensive discussions of paradigms and speakers' use of them, without ever rejecting the term or the concept.

225: 'La langue est une sorte de bric-à-brac ou de Musée Grévin
de la connaissance, et les affinités sémiques ne peuvent pas réflé-
ter une seule vision du monde, car cela supposerait que la langue
n'a pas d'histoire'. Very true, and not only of lexicon; cf. the
equally wise observation of Sapir (1921:105) concerning grammatical
categories but applicable to all facets of linguistic structure:
'It is almost as though at some period in the past the unconscious
mind of the race had made a hasty inventory of experience, commit-
ted itself to a premature classification that allowed of no revision, and saddled the inheritors of the language with a science
that they no longer quite believed in nor had the strength to o-
verthrow'.

I am sure that fifty or a hundred years from now, when the dust
of these battles has settled, the TG movement will — despite the
permanent adoption of some of its features — be regarded as essentially an aberration, a 'swing of the pendulum' (as suggested by
Esper [1968]) which went much too far and needed drastic correc-
tion. Future historians of linguistics will undoubtedly regard
H's book as one of the signs of a turn in the TG tide. We urgently
need either a translation of H's book* or a similar book-length
treatment of TG theories in English.

* [Provided later, under the title *Critical Reflections on
Generative Grammar* (Lake Bluff, Ill.: Jupiter Press, 1981; Edward Sapir Monograph-Series, no. 10.]

CAN LINGUISTICS BE A SCIENCE?

(Lingua 53.221-224 [1981])

This is the question underlying the discussion of Gray (1980), whose basic message is that American linguists (including such diverse types as Leonard Bloomfield, Noam Chomsky and myself) have erred in considering it even possible that linguistics could be a science. The answer of course depends on what is meant by the terms LINGUISTICS and SCIENCE.

In addition to the popular sense of 'polyglottism' ("You're a linguist? How many languages do you speak?'), there are at least three senses in which *linguistics* is used in serious discussion (Hall [1974:227]):

1.   Speculation concerning language in general, from a philosophical or theological point of view.

2.   The description of language for practical purposes.

3.   The application of scientific methods to the study of language.

But what are scientific methods? I have always followed implicitly (though not characterizing it explicitly until Hall [1974:4, fn. 8]) the generally accepted definition of science as

a method for arriving at statements which brook contradiction, concerning only phenomena which are accessible to human observation or are deducible on the basis of observation; whose existence is assumed only on the basis of hypotheses which can be tested, checked, and confirmed or disconfirmed by procedures accessible to all observers, and whose function in the study or discussion of the universe is never considered permanently undeniable or irrefutable.

In Gray (1980:9, 21, 22) "science IN THE STRONG SENSE OF THE TERM" (emphasis mine) or "in the sense that physics is" (22) is mentioned as something that linguistics cannot possibly be, because "the facts of language truly are mentalistic — not physical facts but ideal ones, accessible only, and limited thereby, to human understanding" (22). First of all, notice that not only physics, but any other set of observable phenomena, can be studied by scientific methods as I have just defined them — including not only the structure of the earth (as in, say, geology), but also the actions of living beings, human as well as non-human. The application of scientific method is not confined to those fields in which rigid

quantitative and mathematical analysis can be applied. The procedure of Gray (1980) in insisting that the term *science* be understood only "in the strong sense" is tacitly aprioristic, and involves the rhetorical ploy of the "excluded mean' — i.e., if linguistics cannot be a science "in the sense of that physics is",
it cannot be a science at all.

Of course there are certain phenomena, such as the experiences
of individuals in religion and mysticism, which cannot be replica-
ted and which are therefore not amenable to scientific investigation. Individuals' reports on such experiences can, on occasion,
be of the highest artistic value, as in Dante's *Divine Comedy* and
many other works of literature. Not even the most determined non-
mentalist would deny the benefit to be derived from reading and
analysing such works, nor would he forbid others to undertake such
studies. (He may well do so himself, with Coleridgean "willing
suspension of disbelief".) Spitzer engaged extensively in such
studies, and no-one ever denied him the right to do so.

As for "mentalism" and "mechanism", the debate is largely
(though not wholly) terminological. As just mentioned, many individual experiences take place inside a single person's head (especially the correlation between linguistic sign and non-linguistic
referent which is involved in meaning) and hence are (ast least at
present) inaccessible to objective observation. As I have pointed
out on other occasions (especially in Hall [1972b:1-2], reprinted
in Hall [1978:85-86]), the debate over "mentalism" and "mechanism"
is largely futile, because there are simply not enough data, as
yet, to base our conclusions on. If we use the term MIND to refer
to "what goes on inside a person's head", well and good, but such a
use does not get us any further. Nor does it help to say that the
use of language is "accessible only, and limited thereby, to human
intelligence". Of course it is, and no-one in their senses ever
denied that it was. Its being limited to human intelligence does
not, however, make it *ipso facto* "ideal" in the sense which Spitzer
presumably meant, of being non-physical and permanently inaccessible to objective observation.

In Gray (1980), there are a number of misrepresentations of
both Bloomfield's and my positions. Limitations of space require
me to restrict my examples to one apiece. Bloomfield, we are
told (Gray [1980:11]), after quoting *in extenso* a long foot-note in
Spitzer (1943), does not "discuss or even reply to the arguments
set forth" therein. There was no need for him to do so, since he
had already set forth his criticisms in the preceding pages. I am
wrongly characterized (Gray [1980:21]) as a "transformationalist"
(which I certainly am not, in the Chomskyan sense), simply because
I made use of quite traditional assumptions of ellipsis (omission,
deletion) in such expressions as Italian *un merci* 'a goods (train)'
← *un treno merci*. That I would therefore "be obliged to admit that
some expressions of meaning do not have distinct formal correlates
and that therefore the grammar of a language can never be com-

pletely worked out by starting with form alone" misrepresents my
position entirely. Only a few extremists (Z. S. Harris, Trager,
Bloch) in the 1940's and 1950's ever envisaged such a procedure,
and only in abstract theory at that. I have always been at pains
to point out that starting one's analysis from form does not exclude considerations of meaning, and that inflectional, syntactic,
and semantic criteria must go hand in hand in analysis as they do
in every-one's perception and production of language.

Nor will it do to impose arbitrarily an unrealistically narrow
definition on the term SCIENCE and then accuse the Linguistic Society of America and all American linguists of having formed a
"school" (Gray [1980:2]), simply because the L.S.A. has as its stated purpose "the scientific study of language". As I have repeatedly pointed out in my various discussions of the history of linguistics in North America (collected in Hall [1976], as well as my
reminiscences in Hall [1975c, 1980]), there was a great diversity
in out-look among the numerous American practitioners of linguistics and philology. Refugees from Nazi Germany and other sources
of persecution were welcomed in the 1930's and 1940's, and, when
they behaved like gentlemen, were accepted no matter how "unscientific" their views might be (cf. Hall [1975c:95]). No censorship
was imposed on Spitzer or any-one else.

In the writing of historical "sketches" the back-ground of e-
vents must be taken into account. For decades before the Spitzer -
Bloomfield spat in 1943-44, there had been extensive discussion of
the nature of linguistics and of its status as a science (especially in the journal *Language*). Such important documents as Bloomfield (1926) and Sapir (1929) need to be taken into account for
both the disagreements (which have been over-emphasized in recent
years) and the agreements which they reveal.

The time-sequence of individual clashes is also important. The
exchanges between Spitzer and Bloomfield, and between Bonfante and
myself (as pointed out in Gray [1980:2]) constitute veritable
feuds. It is also quite true that Spitzer "came into American linguistics from the outside" (Gray [1980:2]) — but he, like various
others, came in with an already well-developed persecution-complex
and readiness to turn an intellectual disagreement into an excuse
for initiating a spat, quarrel, or feud. That was his way of
"opening debate". In every instance of his manifold attacks on
American scholars (mostly, though not wholly, younger than himself)
Spitzer was the one to make unmotivated and needlessly hostile criticisms, often (as in the case of his long foot-note to which
Bloomfield took exception) quite out of context. (I have discussed
the back-ground and motivation of both of these feuds in Hall
[1975:37-38, 54-55, 76-77, 81-83, 101-103, 105-106].) Spitzer's polemic attacks were what Malkiel termed, in his obituary of Spitzer
(1960/61:363):

obtrusive footnotes by an uninvited commentator to other scholars'

patient researches; to make things worse, footnotes often colored
by a peevish or sarcastic tone.

(In the references given, both Malkiel and I spoke from first-hand
experience.) In addition to being touchy and quarrelsome, Spitzer
manifested (as pointed out by Malkiel [1960/61:364]):

a deplorable reluctance to grant younger men the same privileges of
independence which he himself had unhesitatingly enjoyed to the
hilt.

One cannot study and evaluate the history of any discipline
using printed sources alone. Such a procedure results in an incomplete, oversimplified, and biased view. If no-one is available to
furnish more details concerning a given historical event or situation, the historian must be aware of the inevitable inadequacy of
his sources. If, however, some-one with first-hand knowledge of
past events can furnish further information and correct misapprehensions, then he or she should do so, as I have tried to do in
this rectification of the misinterpretations contained in Gray
(1980).

REVIEW OF SAMPSON, *LIBERTY AND LANGUAGE*
AND OF MATTHEWS,
GENERATIVE GRAMMAR AND LINGUISTIC COMPETENCE

(Forum Linguisticum 5.274-279 [1980/81])

Liberty and Language. By GEOFFREY SAMPSON. Oxford [England], New
York, Toronto: Oxford University Press, 1979. Pp. viii, 251.
Generative Grammar and Linguistic Competence. By PETER H. MAT-
THEWS. London, Boston, Sydney: George Allen and Unwin, 1979.
Pp. 112.

Both these books are strongly critical of the theories of A. N.
Chomsky, but from very different points of view. Sampson agrees
with some of C's positions in linguistic analysis, but cannot accept C's claims concerning the connection between language and politico-economic considerations. Matthews admired C's earlier work,
but, beginning with his 1967 review of *Aspects*, has not been willing to toe the Chomsky party-line. S is therefore critical of C's
non-linguistic positions, while H rejects certain of his linguistic
theories.

Since their aims are different, their books are not alike in
structure. In a brief introduction (1-12), S inveighs against
"scientism" (1-4), expounds sympathetically C's doctrines regarding
linguistic universals (4-6), and criticizes (6-11) C's use of the
term CREATIVE in what S terms an "impoverished sense" (7). His second chapter interprets C's arguments 'From Linguistics to Anarchism" (13-36) on the basis of "the specific political inferences
Chomsky draws from his own linguistic version of rationalism" (30).
Chapter 3, "Liberalism and Creativity" (37-89) presents S's view of
the (British[1]) liberal ideal in politics, involving a society "in
which patterns of production and distribution of goods are determined by the impersonal mechanism of open competition between individuals acting as free and independent economic agents" (48). This
freedom, S argues, depends on "creativity", interpreted as freedom
and innovation, whereas he views C's anarchico-socialistic doctrines as inherently authoritarian and hostile to freedom (49-59)
and anti-creative, anti-innovative (59). For S, liberalism is
founded on empiricism, socialism on rationalism.

After expounding his views on linguistics and on politics, S
devotes three chapters to criticizing the (according to him, erroneous) conclusion which C draws concerning the latter on the basis
of his brand of the former. In Chapter 4, "Linguistics versus Liberalism" (90-129), S gives his own definition of "creativity" as
"to produce something which falls outside the class implied by any
set of principles that might have been prepared to account for previous examples" (105). He then points out that, in this sense of

the term, C's pronouncements presuppose that the utterance of new
sentences is NOT a creative activity (105). S discusses at considerable length (105-129) the unjustifiable way in which C, with
characteristic "Tarzan-thinking",[2] has confused the issue by
wrongly claiming that human use of language is creative and also
that politico-economic activity is no longer innovative, or "creative" in S's sense. Chapter 5, "Chomsky, race, and foreign policy"
(130-177) is a demonstration that it is Chomskyan rationalism, with
its doctrines of genetic inheritance, that leads to racism and interference in other countries' affairs, rather than (British) liberalism founded on empiricism. "What we know and how we know it" is
the topic of S's sixth chapter (178-209), in which he passes from a
discussion of Skinnerian behaviorism and C's criticisms thereof
(178-186) to a refutation of C's arguments, which, according to S,
are based on a presumed universal validity of people's intuitions
concerning, first their own language, and then their desiderata in
political or economic matters. S contrasts empiricists' readiness
to change their minds, with rationalists' absolutism and *de facto*
support for authoritarianism, Marxist or otherwise.

In his "Conclusion" (210-213), S tells us: "The central aim of
this book has been to show that Chomsky's fine-sounding words about
human nature actually mean something close to the opposite of what
they appear to say. Chomsky calls us creative, and we applaud him;
but if we ask what he means by 'creative', he turns out to mean
what many of us would call 'uncreative'. [...] And this verbal confusion spills over from psychological into verbal discourse. The
proper society for a creative being is a free society, Chomsky
says, and again we applaud. But the kind of 'freedom' which Chomsky has in mind for beings who are 'creative' in his sense is a
'freedom' which many of us would call 'unfreedom'" (210-211).

In contrast to S's book, M's is less than half as long, deals
with a much more restricted problem of specifically linguistic im-
port, and is more tightly organized. It is divided, not into chapters, but into a series of short sections, all of which deal with
the basic problem of the adequacy of generative grammar to cope
with speakers' linguistic competence. In his Introduction (11-22),
M emphasizes that he is restricting his discussion to the subject-
matter of linguistics, as conceived by C (11), and to generative
grammar as a type of formal system (13). Like S, M attacks the i-
dea that linguistics can be a science (11-14), without defining
SCIENCE. In this section and later, M uses a quasi-dialogue form,
imagining objections raised by hecklers and replying to them in an
easy-going, lively colloquial style.

In his substantive discussion, M treats of syntax and lexicon
(25-31), competence (31-40), variation in speech-communities (61-
66), and meaning (66-86). In all these sections, M emphaiszes the
impossibility of establishing sharp definitions and boundaries between phenomena such as would be required for a Chomskyan formalization of grammar to be valid. His last two sections, "Rules and

tendencies" (88-98) and "Grammar and mind" (98-106), contain his
suggestions for modifying our approach to the analysis of language
so as to bring it into accord with observed reality. M would have
us recognize "tendencies" as well as hard-and-fast rules — a basically statistical, probabilistic approach — and abandon the
"black box" or "homunculus" notion of "mind".

     Both S and M have, I think, succeeded in their main aims. S
has demonstrated the invalidity of C's claims that the nature of
human language in any way compels our allegiance to Chomskyan doctrines on politics and economics, based as they are on *Vulgärmarxismus* and Bakuninian anarchism. M has shown that linguistic
structures, in both form and meaning, are too "fuzzy" in themselves, and are too closely tied to variable real-life situations,
to confirm C's view of grammar as casting light on competence.
Both books are well written, with typical English urbanity and
(especially in M's case) wit.

     Neither book, however, is wholly satisfactory. They have two
major defects: ignorance of the nature of science, and neglect of
the history of pre-Chomskyan linguistics. My own definition of
science (based, not on abstract philosophical considerations, but
on direct observation of scientists at work) is:[3]

>   A method for arriving at statements which brook contra-
>   diction, concerning only phenomena which are accessible
>   to human observation or are deducible on the basis of ob-
>   servation; whose existence is assumed only on the basis
>   of hypotheses which can be tested, checked, and confirmed
>   (or disconfirmed) by procedures accessible to all obser-
>   vers; and whose function in the study or discussion of
>   the universe is never considered permanently undeniable
>   or irrefutable.

The methods of scientific investigation, as defined here, are certainly applicable to the study of human activities — linguistic
or non-linguistic — as well as to any other type of phenomenon
observable in the universe we live in, without the necessity of
assuming any other, permanently observable factors to explain them.
M makes this very point with regard to "mentalism", in his final
section, but fails to observe the inconsistency with regard to his
previous denial that linguistics can be a science.

     In neither book will the reader find any but scattered, cursory
references to linguistic analysis done before 1957. Leonard Bloomfield is the only pre-Chomskyan scholar mentioned by both. S also
has references to C. C. Fries (twice), Sapir, Whorf, and Robins
(1967) (once each). M has two other references, to F. de Saussure
and to C. E. Bazell. This is a more serious defect in S than it is
in M, since the latter is concerned with a problem of linguistic a-
nalysis that is much more specifically limited to Chomskyan and
post-Chomskyan theory. On occasion S's neglect of pre-1957 lin-

guistics leads him to perpetrate real howlers, as when he refers (139-140) to Franz Boas as the "father of American linguistics". Did William Dwight Whitney and Maurice Bloomfield never exist? Even in descriptive linguistics, John Wesley Powell, John R. Swanton, and many others worked on American Indian languages long before Boas. The reason Boas is so often cited by American linguists is that he gathered together in one place (Boas [1911]) the evidence collected by himself and many others disproving the universality of Graeco-Latin grammatical categories. S repeats uncritically (103-104) the Chomskyan caricature of the situation in American descriptive linguistics in the 1930's and '40's.[4] He takes at face-value C's claim to have been denied a hearing in the 1950's and early '60's (93).

Central to any discussion of Chomskyan theories is the notorious distinction between competence and performance. Both S and M accept this — more surprising in M's case than in S's, perhaps, because he is concerned with its relation to the formal system of generative grammar. Yet the notion COMPETENCE is itself inadequate. As I have been insisting for some time (beginning with Hall [1958:50-52]), we must distinguish between human CAPACITY to use symbols in general and language in particular, on the one hand, and the KNOW-HOW that each person has with regard to one or more linguistic systems, on the other. Capacity is undoubtedly innate, though we do not know which chromosome or bit of DNA carries it. Know-how, on the other hand, is learned (and, generally, intentionally taught to the growing child in much more complete form than C has been willing to admit[5]). It is perhaps better to avoid the Chomskyan terminology entirely, since it has led to so much confusion, and to speak, instead, of capacity, know-how, and USE. Much of the needless logomachy over "competence" could have been avoided if this distinction had been made from the start — but then C could not have stirred up all the fracas over "innateness".

Paradoxically, although S has seen through the semantic wrenching and "Tarzan-thinking" that underlie C's notions on politics and economics, and the relation of these to language, he has not recognized their presence in C's theories on language itself. At least in part, this is because S does not realize that what he considers new and original in C's theories is anything but new. C's "universals" have their predecessors in the work of such modern theorists as L. Hjelmslev, and of the mediaeval speculative grammarians, particularly the Modistae. "Creativity", no matter how defined, is no startling new discovery on C's part. Croce, Vossler, Spitzer, Sainéan (to mention only a few) have used the same concept; and C's immediate predecessors simply used different terms, such as PRODUCTIVITY or PRODUCTIVE ANALOGY, for the same phenomena. S also seems quite unaware of the dizzying changes in Chomskyan use of such terms as MIND, UNIVERSALS, and SEMANTIC REPRESENTATION. exactly parallel to the variations in the official party-line in Marxist-ruled countries[6] — so much so that non-Chomskyans are beginning to come out and say in print what many of us have been thinking for some time, that TGG "has become an intellectual fraud" (Gray [1977/78:70), if, indeed, it ever was anything else.[7]

Perhaps, though, TGG does have some merits — but if it does, it can make a valid contribution to the analysis of language only if we recognize it, as M says in his final sentence (106), "as one technique of linguistic description, which is especially appropriate for syntax, and not as a model of competence".

NOTES

1. The term LIBERAL of course means something very different in present-day America, in many respects quite the opposite of its British (and earlier American) meaning, as S notes (38 and note 4 thereto on p. 217). For a discussion of the semantic wrenching in such shifts, cf. Robertson (1972 [1976[3]]: 316-325); Hall (1975d).

2. In Hockett's felicitous phrase (1968:63), highly apposite here, though not mentioned by S.

3. Given first in Hall (1974:245, fn. 2). I have cited it to geologists, zoölogists, and botanists, who have expressed agreement and approval.

4. No American linguist ever deliberately limited him- or herself to a narrow corpus, nor is it true that, as S states (103-104), if his description was valid for material outside the corpus, "it was no part of the linguist's intention — if anything, it had to be apologetically explained away". Fries's works on English grammar (1940, 1951) were based on corpora to get, not a restricted body, but as large a body of authentic material as was then available.

5. Cf. Vorster (1975). In Haiti, the *gadò* or baby-tender regularly, from the child's earliest weeks, acts out conversations between herself and the baby, taking both parts and furnishing a model to imitate later (Alfred and Rhoda Métraux, personal communication in 1949).

6. Curiously, S refers (220, fn. 26) to the mafia-like control exerted in many American universities by transformationalists, and cites Anttila (1974) — but fails to draw the obvious conclusions with regard to the TGG party-line.

7. Cf. most recently Gross (1979).

REVIEW OF NEWMEYER, *LINGUISTIC THEORY IN AMERICA*

(Forum Linguisticum 6.177-188 [1981/82])

Linguistic Theory in America: The First Quarter Century of Transformational Grammar. By FREDERICK J. NEWMEYER. New York;
Academic Press, 1980. Pp. x, 290.

What a pathetic book! Obviously intended as a paean of victory
for the school of transformational-generative grammar (TGG), it has
already become notorious for its concluding sentence (250):

> On the basis of this scientific idealization, more
> has been learned about the nature of language in the
> past 25 years than in the previous 2500.

Although devout Chomskyites do not like to admit it, their cause
has by no means been as victorious as Newmeyer and others would
like to imagine. N's book is best viewed as a paradigmatic example
of the dream-world into which the adherents of discredited ideolo-
gies retreat.

N's nine chapters are arranged in chronological order. The
first, "The state of American linguistics in the mid 1960's"
(1-17), follows the usual Chomskyan scenario: Bloomfield and other
linguists had (we are told) a mistaken notion of science, based on
an empiricist approach which denied any relevance to "explanation"
and "resulted in a linguistic description that was nothing more
than a catalogue of observables and statements extractable directly
from observables by a set of mechanical procedures" (5). Almost
the only linguists on whose work N bases these allegations are those
of a narrow group — primarily Z. Harris, and also B. Bloch and the
earlier Charles Hockett. Kenneth Pike, for instance, is mentioned
only in this chapter, and principally as a critic of some views of
the group just mentioned (1, 3, 10, 15-18).

In Chapter 2, "The Chomskyan revolution" (19-59), N gives his
version of the presumed overthrow of structuralism by Chomsky's
work. His description of C's activities is couched in adulatory
terms throughout. He would have us believe, for example, that
"the essence of Chomsky's revolution in linguistics was his gift
to the field of a truly scientific perspective" (20). After sections devoted to C's *Syntactic Structures* (20-33), C himself
(33-35), the antecedents of generative grammar (35-37), generative
phonology (37-32), and language and psychology after C (42-44), we
come to the longest section of the chapter, "Winning the revolu-

tion" (45-59), couched entirely in terms of war-like activity.

The following chapters treat of the changes (described by N as "progress" [61]) in TGG during the 1960's and 1970's: "3. From *Syntactic Structures* to *Aspects of the Theory of Syntax*" (61-92); "4. The late 1960's" (93-132); "5. The Linguistic Wars" (133-173); and "6. Syntax in the 1970s: Constraining the syntactic rules" (175-207). The "linguistic wars" alluded to in Chapter 5 are those between the True Believers who devoutly adhered to Chomskyan orthodoxy and the Heretics of generative semantics, with the victory predictably ascribed to the former (167-172). These chapters, replete with tree-diagrams and similar decorations, are of interest primarily to those who deem the twistings and turnings of the Chomskyan party-line worthy of detailed examination. For those who do not, the only value these chapters have is historical — as an account of the flailings around of the Chomskyites in their efforts to follow the contortions in their guru's thinking.

The two final chapters treat of developments in the late 1970's: "7. On the boundary of formal grammar" (209-226), and "8. Recent developments in syntax and semantics" (227-250). The book ends with a reference-list (251-276), a name-index (277-281), a woefully incomplete general index (283-287), and an "Index of rules and constraints" (289-290).[1]

Now for the book's merits and faults. The former are quickly dealt with, for they do not exist — except, as already said, as documentation of the house-fly-like gyrations of a moribund ideology *in extremis*. The latter, on the contrary, are all-pervasive. They may be divided into sins of omission (e.g. failure to specify the meaning of crucial terms, or to mention objections raised by non-Chomskyites) and of commission (e.g. misrepresentation of facts, semantic distortions, or introduction of irrelevancies).

Exactly what does N mean when he speaks of THEORY, SCIENCE, or SCIENTIFIC IDEALIZATION? He uses these terms all the time, but at no point does he define them. To aid in further discussion, I shall reproduce here (from Hall [1974:245]) my definitions of THEOLOGY and SCIENCE, and shall add a further one of RELIGION. (To avoid misunderstanding, I must emphasize that I have arrived at these definitions by observing the activity of scientists and theologians, rather than by any abstract process of ratiocination.)

> A THEOLOGY is a set of statements brooking no contradiction (DOGMAS), concerning forces or beings (e.g. deities, spirits, devils, souls) which are not accessible to human observation in any controllable or verifiable fashion, but whose existence, paramount importance, and supreme power is assumed *a priori* and is considered an undeniable, irrefutable factor which has to be taken into account as determining everything else in the study or discussion of the universe.

A SCIENCE is a method for arriving at statements which brook contradiction, concerning only phenomena which are accessible to human observation or can be deduced on the basis of observation; whose existence is assumed only on the basis of hypotheses which can be tested, checked, and confirmed (or disconfirmed) by procedures accessible to all observers; and whose function in the study of the universe is never considered permanently undeniable or irrefutable.

A RELIGION is an emotionally based adherence to a theology, unshakable by any evidence obtained from the observation of facts or their analysis by scientific methods.

The term THEORY has a rather broader variation in use, but seems to mean, for most people, "a statement of the abstract principles to be extracted from the observation of some phenomenon". (Note that, contrary to N's statements in his Chapter 1, such observation does not always have to be DIRECTLY confirmed by empirical confirmation, but can also be confirmed indirectly by deductions and extrapolations based on empirically confirmed fact. His quotation [14] from a certain Carl Hempel does not contradict what I have just said.) An IDEALIZATION involves, as pointed out by McCawley (1980:914) "a policy of deciding what factors may be relevant to the phenomena under discussion and ignoring those which one regards as peripheral". But, as McCawley goes on to observe (915), "Idealizations have promissory notes attached to them: a scientific community that accepts an idealization owes the world a satisfactory account of the factors that it is ignoring and is in debt until it or its benefactors in other scientific disciplines produce such accounts and pay off the debt". This is simply a rephrasing of the principle stated long ago by Vaihinger (1924) that fictions may often be profitably introduced into scientific analysis, provided that they and their effects be removed before the analytical process is ended.

Considered in the light of these definitions, Chomskyan doctrines concerning language cut a very sorry figure indeed. (If N or any-one else wishes to object to their being considered in this light, let it be remembered that he offers no definition at all.) The doctrines of TGG are handed down from above, in *a priori* fashion, and are not subject to confirmation or disconfirmation, either directly or indirectly, as in the case of "deep structure", the notorious "language-acquisition-device", or "grammaticality". Chomskyan doctrines are dogmas, the tenets of TGG theology, not the guide-lines of any kind of scientific investigation. He who does not accept them at all is an infidel. He who does accept them becomes a follower of the Chomskyan religion. Like many religions, TGG has had its dizzying changes in dogma, its schisms, its heretics, and its jihads.

Nor can C's "idealizations" be considered in any way scientific.

If a scientist deliberately omits a certain factor from his analysis — e.g. the shape- and density-distribution of heavenly bodies
in celestial mechanics (cited by McCawley [1980:914]), or friction
in calculations of motion — it is in order to obtain a formulation
into which the omitted factor can later be re-inserted and its effects identified. But C's "idealizations" involve the omission of,
not one, but all the features that make human language what it is
— its correlation in each speaker's "mind" with phenomena of the
real world of human experience, i.e. its meaning; its variability,
not only from one speaker to another, but even in each individual's
linguistic system; its social function; and its continual change in
the course of time. As Faust (1970:46) said: "In effect, Chomsky's
ideal speaker-listener is not in a speech-community at all. He is a
lone individual, completely surrounded by mirrors." No such speaker,
devoid of all the normal characteristics of human language, ever
existed or could exist. A phenomenon totally devoid of all its essential features loses its identity. It becomes a zero-phenomenon,
and C's "idealization" of language becomes zero-language.

    C's various "idealizations", such as "deep structure", the
"L.A.D.", and grammaticality, are nothing but fictions, undemonstrable and unnecessary (remember "Occam's razor": *Entia non sunt
multiplicanda praeter necessitatem*), and he never removes them from
his analysis. "Deep structure" does not exist, even in "traces";
there exist only sequences of linguistic forms and their meanings.
So-called "deep structure" is nothing but a reformulation, in terms
of the English SUBJECT + PREDICATE major clause, of the bare bones
of the meaning of an utterance. We need not assume any special
"language-acquisition-device", for, as Putnam (1967), Derwing (1973)
Stemmer (1973) and others have shown, language-learning is simply
part of the general learning-process. "Grammaticality", formulated
in the abstract and on merely logical grounds, does not exist. Like
other linguistic terms, "grammaticality" or "well-formedness" can
be identified only on the basis of statistical frequency and pat-
tern-regularity (cf. Hall [1975]). Grammaticality is, therefore,
inevitably variable from one speaker, one speech-community (small
or large), and one period of time to the next.

    These quite unscientific Chomskyan idealizations have, there-
fore, led C and his disciples to a completely unrealistic and untenable view of language. According to Gray (1977/78:70) "transformational grammar has become an intellectual fraud". One wonders:
has it not always been such? There has been a steady stream of
devastating and conclusive criticism ever since 1957, summarized
(up to 1976) in Hall (1977a)].The volume and intensity of these
criticisms has swelled markedly since 1976. But does N ever mention any criticisms that have come from outside the circle of TGG's
True Believers and Heretics? Only a very few, almost all early
ones from those whom he contemptuously terms the "old guard" structuralists, to answer whom there was "no further need" (20). N's picture (47) of TGG having "so thoroughly won the field" by 1968 that
Hockett's *State of the Art* had no impact and needed no answer is so

unrealistic that it would be tragic, if it were not so ludicrous. In reality, as even N has to admit (250), the TGG field has by now become tremendously fragmented — so fragmented as to lose all unity except that based on the non-existent "foundation which they hold in common -- the recognition that a linguistic theory is a formal model of a speaker's abstract linguistic competence".

Even a favorable critic like McCawley (1980) has pointed out that N's discussion deals, not with linguistic theory as a whole, but only with that of syntax; and that N deals only sketchily with psycholinguistics and neglects wholly several other aspects of linguistic investigation that have important contributions to make to the general theory of language — e.g. dialectology, sociolinguistics, neurolinguistics, sign-language and creolistics. In the study of syntax alone, N makes absolutely no mention of tagmemics, nor indeed of any of the work done by Pike and his students, which is fully as important theoretically as the Chomskyan approach and has given far more valid and useful results in practical application. True, Pike's work has attracted far less public attention than Chomsky's — in part because the Summer Institute of Linguistics has been busy actually doing constructive work instead of publicizing itself, and also because, as Hymes (1964:46, fn. 7) pointed out, a person and a group concerned with missionary work and practical skills enjoys only a marginal position in intellectual politics, and "you can't fight arrogance with humility".

Not only intellectual, but also national and international politics are important in this connection. To read N's presentation, the unwary reader would think that C's doctrines had "won the battle" exclusively on their own merits. However, whatever success they have had is not due to their merits, for, as we have seen, they have none. It is wholly due, as I have pointed out elsewhere (Hall [1980:9-12]), to extraneous factors, chiefly political. Without the turmoil of the 1960's and the ructions over Vietnam, Chomsky's notions would never have achieved notoriety, and they would have received the rejection they deserved (with, perhaps, the preservation of a few useful notational devices). It is worth noting that Lees' naïve rave-review (1957) was the only wholly favorable one that Chomsky (1957) received. The others pointed out the shortcomings of C's approach and the limited basis on which it rested. But N, of course, omits all mention of this crucial factor.

Fully as bad, or even worse, than N's sins of omission are those of commission. Almost since the inception of TGG, it has been recognized (e.g. by Lamb [1967]) that C and his henchmen (I suppose nowadays one should say *henchpersons*) are prone to misrepresenting history, and to maligning any of his predecessors with whose opinions he disagreed, or to praising, no matter how *mal à propos*, any predecessors in whom he thought he detected anticipations of his own doctrine. C's most notorious intellectual malapropism of this kind was his *Cartesian linguistics* (Chomsky [1966a]), whose failings were definitively exposed by a number of experts in that field,

most notably Aarsleff (1970, 1971). True to his principle of men-
tioning almost no non-Chomskyan critics since Hockett (1968), N
passes over this entire aspect of C's *oeuvre* in silence. He follows his guru's lead, however, in misrepresenting historical reality in many respects, often turning it 180° around. Two examples
out of dozens must suffice:

(1) N asserts (47) that Bloch said "Chomsky really seems to be
on the right track. If I were younger, I'd be on his bandwagon
too". In actuality, Bloch's attitude, as reported by a student of
his from first-hand observation, was quite different:

> Bloch, whom I knew well, did NOT encourage TG; he had
> scientific integrity and he told us graduate students
> "this is another way of doing linguistics — I may be
> fossilized for all I know (sarcastic grin) — I am
> anxious to enable you to read in the field for your-
> selves so that you can make up your own minds". This
> is what Bloch actually said — I am one live witness
> to it, you may quote me on it. This is a far cry
> from N's idea that Bloch planted Chomsky's thesis in
> the seminar room. It sat there and gathered dust: we
> read Böhtlingk and Wackernagel to shreds but no one
> (with the exception of ---- ----) ever touched it.

(2) According no N (35), at the 1958 Third Texas Conference
on Problems of Linguistic Analysis of English, in the discussion-
sessions reported in Hill (1962), "we can see linguistic history
docmunented as nowhere else — Chomsky, the *enfant terrible,* taking
on some of the giants of the field and making them look like rather confused students in a beginning linguistics course". All
one needs to do is to read the actual text in Hill (1962) to see
that the exact opposite is true. The other participants tried, in
a friendly fashion, to point out to C the severe limitations to
which his schemes were subject, but he responded (typically) with
a stubborn refusal to entertain any suggestions which did not correspond to his preconceived notions.

Among the many other misstatements of fact, we may cite such
assertions as that "the little syntactic work which was done was,
in a sense, the result of 'cheating' — a complete morphemic analysis had never been worked out even for English" (9). In reality,
Trager and Smith (1951) contained an analysis of English morphology,
as did also Francis (1958). The present reviewer had worked out a
complete morphemic and syntactic analysis for Hungarian (Hall
[1938], wholly revised in 1944) and for Italian (Hall [1948a]). N
also declares arrogantly (20) that "a truly alternative theory [to
C's assumptions] with any credibility has yet to emerge". Since N
confines his discussions entirely to Chomskyan dogma and to his i-
maginary "structuralist" straw-man, he of course does not even mention Pike's tagmemics or Lamb's stratificational theory, which have
not only equal, but greater credibility.

N also manages to misinterpret many of his citations. One ex-

ample must suffice. He quotes (9) Bloomfield's well-known statement (1933a:139) that "in order to give a scientifically accurate
definition of meaning for every form of language, we should have to
have a scientifically accurate knowledge of speaker's world"
[including the complete state of every cell in the speaker's body
— RAHjr.] Then N goes on to state "Since this goal was, of course,
unattainable, recourse to meaning was to be avoided", and then be-
rates Bloomfield for having supposedly been "inconsistent" in constantly bringing meaning-criteria into his analyses.[2] Others (e.g.
Bloch and Z. Harris) did indeed draw this conclusion from Bloomfield's observation, but even then only in theory. Bloomfield himself never advocated the exclusion of meaning from linguistics. He
simply recognized, as every-one should, the inevitably approximate
nature of our apperceptions of meaning (cf. Hall [1972b]) and rightly said (1933a:140) "The statement of meaning is therefore the weak
point in language-study, and will remain so until human knowledge
advances very far beyond its present state". It has, indeed, remained so, despite all the efforts of generative semantics, interpretative semantics, semiotics, etc., just because of the nature of
meaning itself. In every science, there are some facets which are
less amenable to scientific analysis and formulation than others.
We nevertheless have to go ahead and do the best we can, while recognizing (and trying to reduce, as much as possible, by scientific
methods) the limitations under which we work.

We also find semantic distortions. It is well known that, for
the Chomskyites, *explain* means simply "formulate rules for ... ",
and an *explanation* is a rule. (To "explain", say, a passive by
setting up a rule for its transformation from an active is about as
much of an explanation as to say that opium puts people to sleep
because it has a *virtus dormitiva*.) Martin Joos (1958:96) discussed Prague-school phonology in contrast to what he called the
American (Boasian) tradition, using the term *explanation* in quite
a different sense, that of telling WHY sounds had certain characteristics, and regarded a demand for such explanations as unnecessary. Without telling the reader that he is using the word *explanation* in the Chomskyan, not the Joosian, sense, N slanders Joos by
saying (5): "Explanations were not only referred to contemptuously,
but were even made to seem 'un-American'". Joos does not use the
last word in N's sentence, which, in normal use, is pejorative,
implying that the person or doctrine to which it is applied is un-
patriotic and traitorous.[3] There is no justification in Joos' text
for such a gratuitous slur. We could cite many other similar instances of more or less subtle but unsignalled shifts of meaning.

N is quite disingenuous in his attempt to show that TGG is not
as English-based as its critics have maintained. He cites (48) a
number of names of TGG-practitioners who have come to it from the
study of languages other than English, and says that its techniques
have been applied to "literally hundreds of languages" (49). What
he fails to mention is that these applications almost all involve
the imposition of English categories on whatever language is being

dealt with (for a detailed discussion of the TGG analysis of one such language, Thai, cf. Noss [1972]).

The percentage of women engaged in linguistic analysis is hardly relevant to the development of linguistic theory. Yet N devotes about four pages (56-59) to this topic. Here, again, he makes even the most self-contradictory remarks to suit his propagandistic purposes. For instance, he insists (56) that "It is an unfortunate fact that women and racial minorities have not fared much better in linguistics (whether pre- or postgenerative) than in other disciplines" — and then, on the second following page (58), he claims "At the Ph.D. level, women are closing the gap on men more rapidly in linguistics than in academia as a whole". He does not mention the Summer Institute of Linguistics, whose active practitioners include a very high percentage of women — but they are missionaries, and hence of no interest to followers of a hostile ideology.

In his introduction, N states (vii) "Some who know me as a Marxist may be surprised and, perhaps, disappointed that there is no obvious "Marxist analysis" given to the events I describe." Marx's name is indeed not mentioned anywhere; but N's entire approach to the subject is that of an ideologue. Cranston (1974:304) lists five characteristics by which an ideology may be identified:

(1) It contains an explanatory theory of a more or less comprehensive kind about human experience and the external world.

(2) It sets out a programme, in generalized and abstract terms, of social and political organization.

(3) It conceives the realization of this programme as entailing a struggle.

(4) It seeks, not merely to persuade, but to recruit loyal adherents, demanding what is sometimes called commitment.

(5) It addresses a wide public, but may tend to confer some special rôle of leadership on intellectuals.

All we need to do is to substitute "language and its relations with" for "experience" in (1), and "the study of language and hegemony over linguistic societies and journals" for "social and political organization" in (2), to see that Cranston's criteria fit TGG like a glove. Criterion (5) applies, also, in that Chomsky has often made an appeal to the wide public, nurtured on traditional grammar. His appeals have been on only a slightly higher intellectual than that of the late popularizer Mario Pei, but of course the Chomskyites have set themselves up as the discoverers and promulgators of the absolute truth (i.e. whatever the TGG party-line may be at the moment) concerning language. In addition to being a religion, TGG is an ideology, closely modeled on Marxism — or, more exactly, on *Vulgärmarxismus*.

We are living in an age of *Vulgär-----ismen*. Such *gesunkenes Kulturgut* as *Vulgärmarxismus* and *Vulgärfreudianismus* has beset us for a long time. In recent years, a kind of *Vulgärsaussureanismus* has been the only contact with linguistics that the fashionable Parisian intellectualoids and "modern critics" like Roland Barthes and Jacques Derrida have had, filtered through the one-sided approach of Román Jakobson and Claude Lévi-Strauss' further reduction thereof (cf. Hall [1978b]). Chomsky's notion of "linguistics" contains a large dose of *Vulgärmarxismus* and *Vulgäranarchismus*, forced onto the facts of English (and thence onto all other languages). As pointed out by Sampson (1979), C's ideas concerning the relation of language to politics would, if applied, result in destroying freedom and instituting a totalitarian thought- and language-control.

Cranston (1974:196) points out another aspect of ideology:

> It is characteristic of ideology both to exalt action and to regard action in terms of a military analogy. Some observers have pointed out that one has only to consider the prose style of the founders of most ideologies to be struck by the military and warlike language that they habitually use, including words like *struggle*, *resist*, *march*, *victory* and *overcome*; the literature of ideology is replete with martial expressions. In such a view, commitment to an ideology becomes a form of enlistment, so that to become the adherent of an ideology is to become a combatant or partisan.

This observation certainly applies to N's vocabulary and style, which involve the imagery of both military and political conflict. In his Chapter 2, and especially in 2.7 ("Winning the Revolution"), we find repeatedly such words as *campaigner, defend, old guard, rebellion, revolution, struggle, tactic,* and *win victories* from the military sphere, and *charisma, convert* (noun), *hegemony,* and *win over* from the politico-religious.

On occasion, N follows C's lead in introducing — as no honorable scientist would do — politically biased views and statements. Thus, he recognizes (49) the non-linguistic basis for the spread of Chomskyan doctrines in the 1960's by saying "Just as students began *en masse* to question the 'common sense' political assumptions of their upbringing which they felt were rationalizing an imperialistic foreign policy and oppressive domestic policy by the American government, they began to question the 'common sense' pseudoscientific assumptions of empiricism in linguistics". The correlation was certainly there, but the number of students involved (not more than ten percent) was hardly such as to justify the use of the term *en masse*, and the entire falsification of history and the terminology which N uses are obviously Marxist-inspired.

N labors under the delusion that there has been a "Chomskyan revolution" which has already been won. In reality, the TGG-camp is fragmented and its ideology discredited (though still often used as a weapon in academic power-politics[4]). N's attitude is typical of

112 LINGUISTICS AND PSEUDO-LINGUISTICS

autistic self-delusion, a complete withdrawal from the world of reality into a dream-world of wish-fulfillment and megalomania. In
actual fact, TGG never attained, even in the United States, the
status of a Kuhnian "paradigm", and even its former followers find
themselves compelled to renounce their allegiance to it once they
come in contact with the hard facts of real language which do not
jibe with the Chomskyan "idealizations". These latter are the notions which really deserve the adjective *pseudo-scientific*. In
the year before N's book appeared, the journal *Language* published
Gross (1979), with the significant title "On the failure of generative grammar" — as applied even to French, whose syntax is very
close, relatively speaking, to that of English. It is quite significant, also, that of my publications, N makes no mention of Hall
(1977), with its extensive collection of critiques from American
and European scholars. It has often been remarked that C himself
and his disciples are impervious to criticism — an attitude quite
characteristic of schizophrenics who have retreated into an imaginary universe of thought constructed by and for themselves alone.

N's book, clearly intended as a cock-crow of victory from the
summit of a mountain, is in reality a pathetic squawk from the top
of a rubbish-heap. However, his notorious concluding sentence can
still be salvaged by the addition of three little words: [...] more
has been learned about language THAT ISN'T SO in the past 25 years
than in the previous 2500.

NOTES

1. A grumpy aside à propos of this last word: when will people
learn to distinguish between *limitation* (simply the fact of a phenomenon having to exist or take place within boundaries),*restriction*
(its being required to be limited), and *constraint* (the restriction
being imposed by force)?
2. I am reminded of one Italian scholar who chided me for having written on the semantics of the Roumanian neuter, saying that,
since I had studied with Bloomfield, I had no right to deal with
meaning!
3. Similarly, Jakobson (1951) ascribed to me (in Hall [1950c])
the use of this same term, when it is not in my article at all.
4. For instance, a woman linguist, one of the leaders in her
sub-field, and a strong opponent of Chomskyan doctrines, was for
many years denied by promotion and tenure by administrators who
knew no linguistics. Their refusal was in reality on sexist
grounds, but they used as a pretext the fact that she was anti-
Chomskyan. She finally had to have recourse to the courts to obtain justice.

REVIEW OF FIETZ, *FUNKTIONALER STRUKTURALISMUS*

(Western Humanities Review 32.184-186 [1978])

Funktionaler Strukturalismus: Grundlegung eines Modells zur Be-
schreibung von Text und Textfunktion. By LOTHAR FIETZ. Tübingen: Niemeyer, 1976. Pp. xi, 150.

The title of Fietz's book poses an initial problem: what kind
of structuralism is involved? In the last sixty years, there have
been many "structuralisms" in the analysis of both language and literature. Linguistic structuralism began in the nineteenth century, but owes its main development to the posthumous *Cours de linguistique générale* (1917) of Ferdinand de Saussure (1857-1913), as
put together from their lecture-notes (and considerably distorted)
by his disciples Charles Bally and Albert Sechehaye. Saussurean
structuralism involved, *inter alia*, sharp distinctions between
synchronic (descriptive) and diachronic (historical) study of language' between *langue* as a rigid system of abstract relationships
constituting the structure of language, and its concrete realization in actual speech or *parole*; between the collective usage of
the speech-community as part of the *langue*, and the habits of the
individual as mere *parole*; and between the signifier and the
thing signified, with only an arbitrary link between the two
("l'arbitraire du signe").

Later European schools of structural linguistics, such as those
of Prague under the leadership of Prince Nicholas Trubetskoï (1890-
1938) and Román Jakobson (1896-1982); of Copenhagen under Louis
Hjelmslev (1899-1965); and of Paris under André Martinet (1908-   ),
all derive directly or indirectly from Saussure's *Cours*. American structuralism in linguistics, as practised by Edward Sapir
(1884-1939) and Leonard Bloomfield (1887-1949), developed in
large part independently of these European schools. It was characterized by concentration on observable phenomena of linguistic activity and by attention to the social matrix of language. Bloomfield and those influenced by him avoided the *a priori* assumption
of undemonstrable, non-physical "mental" factors, and started
their analysis from linguistic form rather than meaning, without
denying the existence or relevance of the latter.

The French anthropologist Claude Lévi-Strauss (1908-   ) applied a similar structural analysis to the study of primitive society and, together with Jakobson, to that of myths. From this
starting-point, a group of Parisian critics developed what they
termed "structuralism" as applied to literature, combining Lévi-
Straussian analysis of myth with strongly doctrinaire Marxism.

Their successors, a group often called "post-structuralists" or "La Nouvelle Critique", including the late Roland Barthes, Gérard Genette, and Jacques Derrida, have substituted "hermeneutic" (i.e. personal and emotional) analysis for that of "structure", but continue their predecessors' Marxism. The philosophically oriented pseudo-linguistics of A. N. Chomsky (a strong critic of American structuralism) has been integrated by these Parisian critics into their system, especially the concept of "deep structure".

In his book, Fietz is essentially attempting to rescue the structural analysis of literature from the clutches of the Parisian Marxists. In Part I (Chapter I, pp. 1-28), he sketches briefly the history of the various structuralisms. He emphasizes the need for objective study of a work of literature, not exclusively in and for itself, but in its function as related to the intellectual and cultural milieu in which it developed. Part II contains two chapters, of which the first (pp. 29-48) discusses "thematic deep structure as the determiner of the choice and organization of signs", and the second (pp. 49-70) "the rhetorical surface structure as a function of deep structure". In the third part, two further chapters establish "the theoretical basis for a functional-structuralistic model for describing the function of a text", with one of them on "the scientific premises of the description of textual function: the text as an instrument for the achievement of effects" (pp. 71-86), and another on "textual strategies as procedures for achieving effects" (pp. 87-129). The fourth part is again coterminous with a single chapter (no. VI, pp. 131-154), on the practical application of Fietz's principles as exemplified in the relation between the structure of the English novel and its readers' expectations as they developed throughout its history. Two indices of names (pp. 155-160) and of topics (pp. 157-160) complete the book.

Fietz knows well the history and methods of the various linguistic and literary structuralisms, and uses whatever techniques of analysis will serve his purpose. He rightly emphasizes the deficiencies of a rigidly descriptive approach, insisting that we need as extensive as possible a knowledge of cultural history, to understand the function which a given work of literature fulfilled for its readers, as well as the (often quite different) function it may have acquired later. To determine a work's function, we must know what its readers, in any given period, expected, and what effects its writer aimed at producing. We can discover these factors, according to Fietz, by analysing the signs the author uses, again taking them in their historical context. Social and political factors are to be taken into account, but not made an aprioristic basis for analysis, and literary criticism is not to be made the servant of any political doctrine. Fietz thus restores several necessary dimensions which have been lost in the rigidly historical, doctrinaire, and politicized pseudo-structuralism of the Parisian Marxist cliques, and also in the egocentric, solipsistic flights of irresponsible, uncontrolled free-associationistic criticism of the "Nouvelle Critique" school à la Derrida.

Two unfortunate features of Fietz's book must be mentioned. Chomsky's terms DEEP STRUCTURE and SURFACE STRUCTURE have become very popular, although they correspond to no observable or deducible realities in language. (There exist only linguistic FORMS; the real-life phenomena to which they refer, i.e. their REFERENTS; and the correlation between a form and its referent, i.e. its SENSE.) As Fietz uses the term DEEP STRUCTURE, it refers simply to the basic message of a passage or of an entire work, and SURFACE STRUCTURE is the passage or work in its totality. Fietz's SIGNS are the "key-words" which give the reader or hearer a clue to the basic message. It would have been better to avoid these meaningless Chomskyan slogans and to use terms with clear reference instead.

The other objectionable feature of Fietz's book is his style. His German is convoluted and prolix, and packed with lexical borrowings from English, French, Latin, and Greek. Perhaps it would have been better to have written the book in either English or French. The standard scholarly style of the latter language, especially, would have enforced clarity of expression and would have reached an audience which is in particular need of such a reorientation.

Pay attention to history; consider the individual author and his aims in relation to his reader's expectations; analyse the means by which these aims are made to correspond to effects a-achieved — none of these precepts is exactly new in literary analysis. The now almost forgotten manuals of Nitze and Dargan, and of Lanson for French literature, or those of Taine and of Legouis and Cazamian for English, were based on exactly these principles. To a certain extent, it may seem as if Fietz is rediscovering the wheel. However, when it has become fashionable for a gullible public to let themselves be duped into throwing away their wheels and buying square blocks to put on their vehicles, it is time for someone to point out anew the merits of round wheels.

DECONSTRUCTING DERRIDA ON LANGUAGE

(*Tra linguistica storica e linguistica generale*
107-116 [Pisa, Pacini, 1985])

In recent years, an approach to literature called DECONSTRUC-
TION has become wide-spread, especially among North American critics. It is based on the doctrines propounded by the philosopher
Jacques Derrida, especially in his *De la grammatologie* (1967a), and
such further works as *L'écriture et la différence* (1967b) and *La
dissémination* (1972).[1] In these, he sets forth a group of doctrines concerning language, and especially the relation of writing
(*l'écriture*) to speech, which are widely at variance with the findings of both descriptive and historical linguistics, but which
serve as the basis for his increasingly influential views on literature. Derrida's basic purpose is to "deconstruct", i.e. to des-
troy, to demolish,[2] the Western philosophical and literary tradition by turning prevailing concepts of language and its relation to
thought upside down. It is my aim in this discussion to "deconstruct" Derrida's notions, in their turn, by showing their lack of
foundation in what is known about language from valid linguistic
study.

Derrida's main theses concerning language are:

1. Writing is not only equal to speech, but anterior
and primary in importance and historical origin;

2. The Saussurean doctrine[3] of "l'arbitraire du signe"
is unfounded, since "l'écriture" is not arbitrary;

3. Undue emphasis on writing as a secondary representation of speech has grown out of "phonocentrism" and
"logocentrism";

4. This "logocentrism" has been a type of ethnocentrism, serving as a vehicle for Western "imperialism"
in the rest of the world;

5. The "signifiant" is opaque and the "signifié" is
thereby inaccessible to complete understanding or interpretation;

6. It is therefore not possible to analyze a text except in relation to itself;

7. Discussion of a work of literature must therefore
be aimed at "deconstructing" its layers of signification
until its internal inconsistencies are revealed, leading
to an "aporia" or impossibility of determining its true
meaning because of the presence of mutual contradictions.

Not one of these Derridian doctrines will stand up under critical analysis, His central thesis, that writing is anterior to speech, and that the latter is simply one aspect of the former, is set forth in Derrida (1967a), in an aprioristic, authoritarian fashion, in teneral terms (I, ch. 1) and then in a lengthy polemic against Saussure (I, ch. 2), Lévi-Strauss (II, ch.1), and Rousseau (II, ch.s 2-4). From the outset of the discussion, Derrida presents his doctrines as if these three men and all others who consider writing secondary to speech were flying in the face of a self-evident truth, but he cites no evidence in support of his position. In fact, however, there are four considerations, all well attested in the extensive body of linguistic studies, which point to the priority of speech:

(A) Its universality. All humans live in speech-communities, speaking and responding to speech, whereas relatively few languages (only a couple of thousand out of the six or seven thousand spoken throughout the earth) are accompanied by any sort of writing-system.

(B) The length of time which must have been involved in its development. There is no such thing as a structurally "primitive" language.[4] Enough languages have been studied by now for us to know that they all have reached approximately comparable stages of development.[5] Furthermore, we know that, as far back as one can go in language-history through documentation and reconstruction of proto-languages, there has been no substantial change in the stage of development reached.[6] Language does change, but only very slowly and gradually. For human language to have reached its present stage, therefore, many tens of thousands of years must have been required. Writing, however, as is well known,[7] is a development of the last six thousand years or so.

(C) The ontogeny of language in individual humans. Each normal person learns, first to respond to heard speech, and then to speak, at a very early age (one to three years), and does so unreflectingly.[8] Reading and writing, however, are always learned later (in our society, normally not before the age of four or five at the earliest), and almost always as a conscious process. Hence our practically universal concentration of attention on language as it is written rather than as it is spoken, and the very wide-spread delusion that "written language" is on a par with "spoken language". It is on this attitude,[9] of course, that Derrida relies for the acceptance of his even more radical thesis of the priority of writing. ("After all, why not?" is likely to be the attitude of the ordinary naïve literate person.)

(D) The universal, but almost universally neglected, fact that no reading or writing goes on without at least some speech-activity taking place in the reader's or writer's brain. Whenever any-one reads or writes, there is always some speech-activity in the brain and central nervous system, at the level of neural impulses, which can be measured by electromyograms[10] and which arrive at the muscles of the organs of speech. Unsophisticated readers and writers speak wholly or partially out loud. Sophisticated persons learn to suppress the nervous impulses at the muscular level — but they keep on sub-vocalizing all the same. This is true of rapid readers as well as of slow ones: in reading rapidly, the peruser of the printed text skips from one high point to the next, extrapolating from the words he has actually read to what lies in between.

In view of these considerations, it cannot possibly be maintained that writing is anterior to or includes speech as part of itself, unless the term WRITING is given a wildly different meaning from its usual one. This is exactly what Derrida does, casually and parenthetically: after over fifty pages in which he has been using the term *écriture* in two senses, without informing the reader that he is doing so, he finally says (1967a:65):

> Si "écriture" signifie inscription et d'abord institution durable d'un signe (et c'est le seul noyau irréductible du concept d'écriture) l'écriture en général couvre tout le champ des signes linguistiques.

By thus redefining *écriture* or *writing*, however, Derrida is reducing his entire thesis to a *vérité de La Palisse*. Since language as spoken is a system of signs (better, as we shall see later, of symbols), of course it forms part of the wider context of human communication by means of both linguistic and non-linguistic signs. Whoever said it didn't, and why all the fuss?[11]

After finally admitting, in a parenthetical and unobtrusive way, that he is really extending the term *écriture* far beyond its usual meaning, Derrida occasionally refers to the extended sense with the term *archi-écriture*, but normally continues to use the simplex, now in one sense and now in another. This is a procedure which might be termed *logomanganeia* 'word-juggling', verbal sleight-of-hand', and which I have called elsewhere[12] 'semantic wrenching'. It involves the (mostly unacknowledged) sudden use, in an unaccustomed sense, of a term which has a normal meaning familiar to all speakers of a language. Confusion and disorientation are thus caused among hearers or readers unless they are on their guard.

In discussing Saussure's and others' recognition of the "arbitrary" (unmotivated, non-iconic) nature of the "linguistic sign", Derrida falls into the same error as they do, of not distinguishing adequately between sign, signal, and symbol. The mediaeval formulation of a sign, *aliquid stat pro aliquo*, is insufficient. We must distinguish between a SIGN (e.g. fragrant warm air coming from the kitchen as an indication that Mother is preparing dinner), a SIGNAL (such as a traffic-light, indicating that some specific act is being performed or to be performed), and a SYMBOL (a given phenomenon closely correlated with another, e.g. a flag symbolizing a

country).[13] Of course there are non-linguistic and especially visual symbols, in fact sets of symbols (such as the European road-
sign-system[14]) used in human communication; but these are all less
complex and less universally serviceable than oral-auditory linguistic systems of symbolism, i.e. languages.

At some early stage of human development, there may well have
been competition between visual and auditory symbols, on a relatively elementary level. The latter clearly won out for functions
of basic communication, for obvious reasons, especially perceptibi-
lity in the dark and leaving the hands free.[15] All systems of visual symbolism are incomplete and inadequate for human communication
as a whole. In some instances, e.g. mathematics and formal logic,
written symbols can indeed extend the range of certain types of
formulation beyond that of normal language.[16] Even in such instances, however, the systems thus extended have their roots in ordinary speech, and are dependent on it, not vice versa.[17] It is
thus clear that Derrida's contention (1967a: I, ch. 1) that the age
of "phonocentrism" is over and that "écriture" (in any sense) is
bound to be the "wave of the future" is unfounded.

Derrida's insistence on the "opacity of the linguistic sign" is
like-wise unjustified. Like virtually all who follow the mediaeval,
Cartesian, and Saussurean tradition of semantic analysis, he accepts and uses unquestioningly the binary opposition of "signifiant" and "signifié". This formulation of the nature of meaning is,
as I have pointed out elsewhere,[18] unsatisfactory. What is custom-
arily termed MEANING involves a correlation between sequences of
functional units of sound (phonemes) grouped in morphemes, syntag-
mata or lexemes, on the one hand, and what they refer to in the
world in which we live and have our experiences, on the other.
(The "ultimate reality" of our lives and experiences is irrelevant
here: we all act and speak AS IF they were real, for purposes of e-
very-day living, and this is all that counts in our consideration
of normal — including literary — language.) But there is a
third, intermediate aspect of this process: this correlation between linguistic form and its referent takes place only in the
"mind" (however we define this term) of each individual speaker.

All "meanings", "ideas", and "concepts", therefore, have their
locus existendi only in the brains and central nervous systems of
individual humans. Because of the varying situations in which language and its elements have to be used, these correlations between
linguistic forms and their referents must necessarily be at least
slightly loose, in each individual and from one individual to the
next.[19] No normal language is a completely tight, "well-formed"
system.[20] (On the other hand, of course, the exigencies of normal
every-day social contact keep meanings fairly close to one another
in the usage of the members of a speech-community.) Absolute semantic rigor can be found only in arbitrarily limited systems where
it is useful, such as those of mathematics, formal logic, computer-
"languages", and the like. It is therefore unrealistic to expect

any type of discourse, whether literary or not, to be free of illo-
gicalities and at least slight contradictions. All too often, the
deconstructive search for "aporía" serves simply as an excuse for
logogoeteia, intellectually meretricious verbal razzle-dazzle (e.g.
in Derrida 1967b, 1972, etc.).

Derrida's readers can get from his discussions of linguistics
only a very incomplete and inadequate idea of its contributions to
the problems he is treating. His extensive discussions of Plato
and Rousseau are beside the point, since their pre-scientific
views on language are of only historical interest. Equally irrelevant are the dicta of the many philosophers whom Derrida discusses
(e.g. Kant, Nietzsche, Husserl, Heidegger, etc.), who deal with
terminological problems but not those of linguistic structure. Of
modern linguists, the only one he discusses extensively is Saussure
(in the least sound aspects of the *Cours*). He pays some attention
to Hjelmslev and the Copenhagen school (1967a:64, n. 7; 86-87; 283-
291; 293) and makes mention here and there of Trubetskoï (1967a:
64, n. 7), Jakobson (1967a:64, n. 7; 93-94; 101-102; 105-106), and
Martinet (1967a:80-82). Leonard Bloomfield is mentioned only once
(1967a:73), where Derrida repeats the old canard of Bloomfield and
his followers having supposedly banned the study of meaning from
linguistics. Of the sound foundation provided for linguistics by
such scholars as Whitney (1875), Sapir (1921), Bloomfield (1933a),
and Pike (1967[2]), there is absolutely no mention.

Derrida's arguments against "logocentrism" are shot through
with irrelevancies used for polemic purposes. We have already mentioned his politically based charges of "ethnocentrism" and "imperialism" supposedly inherent in alphabetic writing (e.g. 1967a:11,
12, 117, etc.). He uses such emotionally loaded terms as *violence*
and *viol* 'rape' in connection with Lévi-Strauss's efforts to explain the use of writing to the Nambikwara (1967a:164-165). His
definitions are often unmotivated and arbitrary, as we have seen
in the case of *écriture*, or in his restriction (1972:71) of the
term TEXT:

> Un texte n'est un texte que s'il cache au premier re-
> gard, au premier venu, la loi de sa composition et la
> règle de son jeu.

This is another of Derrida's wilful semantic wrenchings: what he is
really saying here is simply that he himself is not interested in
any text which is not "opaque" and difficult to construe. (For a
linguist, a text is any stretch of discourse, short or long, oral
or written.) The lowest point is reached where, in one of his irrelevant introductions of *Vulgärfreudianismus*, he identifies par-
ticipation in conversation (*le colloque*) with "l'auto-affection
sexuelle", i.e. masturbation (1967a:236-237).

In connection with the unfortunate feud in English universities
between the "language" and the "literature" sides, Tolkien (1959)

made the highly important distinction between PHILOLOGY, the love
of words and language, and MISOLOGY, the hatred of words and language. He says (1959:225) "Philology is the foundation of humane
letters; 'misology' is a disqualifying defect or disease". In Tol-
kienian terms, the "deconstructionists" are misologists. They hate
language, they hate words, and treat them only as play-things or
worse, to be twisted out of their natural shape and meaning and to
be played nasty games with (as do Tolkien's orcs in *The Lord of
the Rings*).

For the English scholar George Watson (1982), the school of "La
Nouvelle Critique" (Derrida, Barthes, Genette, *et hoc genus omne*)
is a "dinosaur", already on the way to becoming extinct in its
home-land, sinking into the mire because of its own weight and
sluggishness. Unfortunately, the same cannot be said of the situation in North America. Watson (1982:63) quotes Valéry's dictum
"Tout s'achève en Sorbonne", and then remarks "Since the French are
now bored with La Nouvelle Critique, perhaps Valéry should have remarked that everything fetches up in New Haven; it is Yale that mi-
mics a master that is no longer there". He could have gone even
farther: unfortunately, Yale is in its turn mimicked by sub-colo-
nies in various other North American universities. "Deconstructionism" furnishes endless opportunities for endless *logomanganeia*
in endless Ph.D.-theses. It, like transformational-generative
grammar, is one of those games at which "any number may play, no
previous experience required".

The best antidotes to these Derridian aberrations are Pike
(1982) and Ong (1982). The latter contains a sound and well-argued
discussion of the relation between orality and oral-based culture,
on the one hand, and writing, with its cultural and intellectual
results, on the other. Ong (1982:121,129) rightly speaks of "Derrida's on-going logomachy with the text". In the study of literature, it is time to get away from Derridian *logomanganeia* and *logogoeteia*, which give rise only to solipsistic ego-trips masquerading
as criticism, and to return to the only valid purpose of secondary
discussion of literature, that of making a text clearer and more
easily understandable to the reader.

NOTES

1. Cf. also the expositions of his doctrines in Accame (1976);
Culler (1982); Leitch (1982); Morris (1982).
2. He uses the term *déconstruction* most frequently, but also
occasionally *démolition* and *destruction* as synonyms thereof. The
basic meaning of *déconstruction* to be gathered from a study of his
usage is 'analysis with negative intent'.
3. As set forth in the posthumous *Cours de linguistique générale* (1916), prepared from lecture-notes by his students Charles
Bally, Albert Sechehaye, and Albert Reidlinger. It has been shown
(especially by Godel [1957]) that this version is far from reliable.
4. All attempts to interpret one language-structure or another

as "primitive" or reflecting "savage" mentality have failed, as
did, for instance, Sommerfelt's faulty analysis (1938) of Arunta,
a language of central Australia, as shown by Strehlow (1948) and
Laycock (1960).

    5. Cf. the lapidary formulation of Sapir (1921:234): "When it
comes to linguistic form, Plato walks with the Macedonian swine-
herd, and Confucius with the head-hunting savage of Assam".

    6. The only way to avoid this conclusion is to assume a sudden
leap, at some unspecified time, from non-use to use of fully developed language; but there is no evidence to support such a "crea-
tionist" assumption. Exactly what time-span must have been required, or what specific stages were passed through, no-one can say
for sure, although many efforts have been made, e.g. most recently,
on an anthropological basis, by Wescott (1980), and, on a philosophical basis, by Gans (1981).

    7. Cf. any history of writing, e.g. Diringer (1953, 1962), or
Gelb (1952 [1963^2]).

    8. Cf. the extensive literature on children's language-learn-
ing.

    9. Cf. my discussion of this matter in Hall (1975b), reviewing
Vachek (1973).

    10. This phenomenon has been well documented by experimental
psychologists. The classical reference is now Edfeldt (1960).

    11. Cf. Ong's critique (1982:94) of Derrida's extension of the
term WRITING: " [...] investigations of writing which take 'writing' to mean any visible or sensible mark with an assigned meaning
merge writing with purely biological behavior. [...] Using the
term 'writing' in this extended sense to include any semiotic marking trivializes its meaning".

    12. Hall (1975d), reviewing Dàrdano (1973).

    13. For an excellent brief discussion, cf. Chao (1968:194-227).

    14. Cf. Buyssens (1943).

    15. Cf. Hockett (1973:379-380).

    16. Cf. Chao (1968:122, 198-200).

    17. Cf. Hockett (1968:266; 1973a:657-658).

    18. Hall (1972b); cf. also Hockett (1958: ch. 18; 1973:105).

    19. Cf. the discussion of universal looseness of correlation
between form and referent in Laughlin (1973:4-12). Only persons
brought up on the unrealistic notion that language has to be exact,
precise, and wholly logical would be upset on finding that it virtually never is so.

    20. Cf. Hockett (1968: ch. 3).

REFERENCES

1. ABBREVIATIONS

AA	American Anthropologist
AcLHa.	Acta Linguistica Hafniensia
AGI	Archivio Glottologico Italiano
ASLU	Acta Societatis Linguisticae Upsaliensis
ASNS	Archiv für das Studium der neueren Sprachen
BSLP	Bulletin de la Société de Linguistique de Paris
ESMS	Edward Sapir Monograph Series
FolL	Folia Linguistica
ForL	Forum Linguisticum
FouL	Foundations of Language
HAIL	Handbook of American Indian Languages
HiL	Historiographia Linguistica
IF	Indogermanische Forschungen
IJAL	International Journal of American Linguistics
JEAB	Journal of the Experimental Analysis of Behavior
JL	Janua Linguarum
JL-SC	Janua Linguarum, Series Critica
JL-SMa.	Janua Linguarum, Series Major
JL-SMi.	Janua Linguarum, Series Minor
JL-SP	Janua Linguarum, Series Practica
LSc.	Language Sciences
MLJ	Modern Language Journal
NM	Neuphilologische Mitteilungen
PRM-CLS[n]	Proceedings of the [n] Regional Meeting of the Chicago Linguistic Society
RPh.	Romance Philology
Trends Vol.	J. Whatmough and C. Mohrmann (eds.): Trends in European and American Linguistics, Volume 1. Utrecht – Antwerp: Spectrum, 1961.

2. AUTHOR, DATE, AND TITLE LISTINGS

Aarsleff, Hans. 1970. The history of linguistics and Professor Chomsky. Language 46.570-585.
———. 1971. Cartesian linguistics: history or fantasy? LSc. 17.1-12.
———. 1974. The tradition of Condillac: the problem of the origin of language in the eighteenth century and the debate in the Berlin Academy before Herder. In Hymes (ed.) 1974:93-156.
Accame, Lorenzo. 1976. La decostruzione e il testo. Firenze:

Sansoni Nuova.
Andersen, Henning. 1969. Lenition in Common Slavic. Language
    45.553-574.
Anttila, Raimo. 1972. An introduction to historical and compara-
    tive linguistics. New York and London: MacMillan.
————. 1974. Revelation as linguistic revolution. First LACUS
    Forum 171-176.
Austin, William Mandeville, Jr. 1967. Logicalism and formalism
    in linguistics. In W. M. Austin, Jr. (ed.): Papers in lin-
    guistics in honor of Léon Dostert 15-22 (The Hague: Mouton,
    1967; JL-SMa. no. 25.)
Bach, Emmon. 1964. Introduction to transformational grammars.
    New York: Holt, Rinehart and Winston.
———— and Robert T. Harms (eds.). 1969. Universals in linguis-
    tic theory. New York: Holt, Rinehart and Winston.
Barnhart, Clarence, L., Sol Steinmetz, and Robert K. Barnhart.
    1973. The Barnhart dictionary of new English since 1962.
    Bronxville and New York: Barnhart / Harper and Row.
Battisti, Carlo, and Giovanni Alessio. 1950-57. Dizionario eti-
    mologico italiano. Firenze: Barbèra.
Baugh, Albert Croll. 1935. A history of the English language.
    New York and London: Appleton-Century. [2nd ed., 1957.]
Behre, Frank. 1967. Studies in Agatha Christie's writings: the
    behaviour of a *good* (*great*) *deal*, a *lot*, *lots*, *much*, *plenty*,
    many, a *good* (*great*) *many*. Göteborg: Elanders Boktryckeri.
Benoit, Leroy James. Forthcoming. Cartesian linguistica: a
    protest.
Benveniste, Emile. 1946. Structure des relations de personne
    dans le verbe. BSLP 43:1.1-12.
Bernstein, Leonard. 1976. The unanswered question. Cambridge
    (Mass.): Harvard University Press.
Bierwisch, Manfred. 1966. Notice of Proceedings of the Ninth In-
    ternational Congress of Linguists. Germanistik 7.15-17.
————. 1971. Modern linguistics: its development, methods and
    problems. The Hague: Mouton. (JL-SMi. no. 110.)
Bloch, Bernard, and George L. Trager. 1942. Outline of linguis-
    tic analysis. Baltimore: Linguistic Society of America.
Bloomfield, Leonard. 1914. Introduction to the scientific study
    of language. New York: Holt. [New ed., Amsterdam, 1983.]
————. 1925. Why a Linguistic Society? Language 1.1-5. Re-
    printed in Hockett (ed.) 1970:109-112.
————. 1926. A set of postulates for the science of language.
    Language 2.143-164. Reprinted in Hockett (ed.): 1970:128-138.
————. 1933a. Language. New York: Holt.
    Spanish translation: Lenguaje. Lima, Perú: Universidad Nacional
    Mayor de San Marcos, 1961.
    Italian translation: Il linguaggio. Milano: Il Saggiatore, 1974.
————. 1933b. The structure of learnèd words. A Commemorative
    Volume Issued by the Institute for Research in English Teach-
    ing on the Occasion of the Tenth Annual Conference of English
    Teachers 17-23 (Tokyo). Reprinted in Hockett (ed.)
    1970:252-256.

————. 1944. Secondary and tertiary responses to language. Language 20.45-55. Reprinted in Hockett (ed.): 1970:413-425.

————. 1945. On describing inflection. Monatshefte für deutschen Unterricht 37:4/5.8-13.

————. 1946. Twenty-one years of the Linguistic Society. Language 22.1-5. Reprinted in Hockett (ed.) 1970:491-494.

Boas, Franz. 1911. Introduction. HAIL 1.1-83.

————. 1911-35. Handbook of American Indian languages. Washington, D. C.: Bureau of American Ethnology. 3 vols.

Bolinger, Dwight L. 1960a. Syntactic blends and other matters. Language 37.366-381.

————. 1960b. Linguistic science and linguistic engineering. Word 16.374-389.

————. 1967. The imperative in English. To Honor Román Jakobson 1.355-362. (The Hague: Mouton [JL-SMa. no. 31].)

————. 1976. Meaning and memory. ForL 1.1-14.

Bracken, Harry M. 1972. Chomsky's Cartesianism. LSc. 22.11-17.

Brekle, Herbert. 1964. Semiotik und linguistische Semantik in Port-Royal. IF 69.103-121.

———— (ed.). 1966. Lancelot, Claude, and Antoine Arnauld: Grammaire générale et raisonnée de Port-Royal. Stuttgart - Bad Cannstatt: Frommann-Holzboog. 2 vols.

————. 1967. Die Bedeutung der Grammaire générale et raisonnée — bekannt als Grammatik von Port Royal — für die heutige Sprachwissenschaft. IF 72.1-21.

————. 1969. Generative semantics vs. deep syntax. In F. Kiefer (ed.): Studies in Syntax and Semantics 80-90 (Dordrecht: Reidel).

Brunot, Ferdinand. 1913. Histoire de la langue française, vol. 4. Paris: Colin.

Buyssens, Eric. 1943. Les langages et le discours. Bruxelles: Office de Publicité.

————. 1969. La grammaire générative selon Chomsky. Revue Belge de Philologie et d'Histoire 47.840-857.

Camilli, Amerindo. 1965. Pronuncia e grafia dell'italiano. 3rd ed., rev. P. Fiorelli. Firenze: Sansoni.

Chafe, Wallace. 1968. Idiomaticity as an anomaly in the Chomskyan paradigm. FouL 4.109-127.

————. 1970. Meaning and the structure of language. Chicago: University of Chicago Press.

Chao, Yuen Ren. 1968. Language and symbolic systems. Cambridge (Eng.): Cambridge University Press.

Chassang, A. (ed.). 1880. Claude Favre de Vaugelas: Remarques sur la langue française. Paris: Cerf.

Chevalier, Jean C. 1967. La Grammaire générale de Port-Royal et la critique moderne. Langages 7.16-33.

Chomsky, Avram Noam. 1957a. Syntactic structures. The Hague: Mouton. (JL, no. 4.)

————. 1957b. Review of Hockett (1955). IJAL 23.223-234.

————. 1959. Review of Skinner (1957). LAnguage 35.26-58.

————. 1962. Explanatory models in linguistics. Logic, Methodology and Philosophy of Science 529-550 (Stanford, California:

126   LINGUISTICS AND PSEUDO-LINGUISTICS

Stanford University Press).

———. 1964a. Current issues in linguistic theory. The Hague: Mouton. (JL-SMi. no. 38.)

———. 1964b. The logical basis of linguistic theory. Proceedings of the Ninth International Congress of Linguists, 914-978 (The Hague: Mouton).

———. 1965. Aspects of the theory of syntax. Cambridge (Mass.): M.I.T. Press. Paper-back edition, 1969.

———. 1965/66. The current trend in linguistics: present directions. College English 27.587-595.

———. 1966a. Cartesian linguistics. New York: Harper and Row.

———. 1966b. Topics in the theory of generative grammar. In Sebeok (ed.) 1966:1-60.

———. 1967a. The responsibility of intellectuals. New York Review of Books 8:3.16-26.

———. 1967b. The general properties of language. In C. H. Millikan and F. L. Darley (eds.): Brain Mechanisms Underlying Speech and Language 73-81, with discussion 81-88 (New York: Grune and Stratton).

———. 1968. Language and mind. New York: Harcourt, Brace and World.

———. 1970. Remarks on nominalization. In R. Jacobs and P. Rosenbaum (eds.): Readings in English Transformational Grammar 184-221 (Waltham, Mass.: Ginn and Co.).

——— and Morris Halle. 1968. Sound patterns of English. New York: Harper and Row.

Christie, William M., Jr. 1976. Another look at classical phonemics. LSc. 39.37-39.

Cognet, Louis. 1950. Claude Lancelot, solitaire de Port-Royal. Paris: Sulliver.

Collinder, Björn. 1970. Noam Chomsky und die generative Grammatik: eine kritische Betrachtung. ASLU NS.2:1.

Coseriu, Eugenio. 1957. Logicismo y antilogicismo en el lenguaje. Revista Nacional (Montevideo) 189.45-473. Also separately, Montevideo, 1958. Reprinted in Coseriu: Teoria del lenguaje y lingüística general 235-260 (Madrid: Gredos, 1962).

———. 1969. Semantik, innere Sprachform und Tiefenstruktur. Tübingen: Romanisches Seminar der Universität.

Cranston, Maurice William. 1974. Ideology. Encyclopaedia Britannica 9.194-198.

Croce, Benedetto. 1902. Estetica come scienza del linguaggio e linguistica generale. Bari: Laterza.

Culler, Jonathan. 1982. On deconstruction: theory and criticism after structuralism. Ithaca, N.Y.: Cornell University Press.

Danielsen, Niels. 1971. Das generative Abenteuer. Språklike Bidrag 6:26 (Lund).

———. 1973. Plaidoyer gegen die generative Tiefenoperationen: Kritik einer Scheinlehre. ASNS 20.241-262.

Dàrdano, Maurizio. 1973. Il linguaggio dei giornali italiani. Bari: Laterza.

Davis, Martin. 1958. Computability and unsolvability. New York: McGraw-Hill.

Derrida, Jacques. 1967a. De la grammatologie. Paris: Seuil.
——. 1967b. L'écriture et la différence. Paris: Seuil.
——. 1972. La dissémination. Paris: Seuil.
——. 1978. Glas. Paris: Seuil.
Derwing, Bruce L. 1973. Transformational grammar as a theory of language acquisition: a study in the empirical, conceptual and methodological foundations of contemporary linguistic theory. Cambridge (England): Cambridge University Press.
Devoto, Giàcomo. 1964. Review of Hall (1963). Lingua Nostra 25.26.
Dik, Simon C. 1967. Some critical remarks on the treatment of morphological structure in transformational generative grammar. Lingua 18.358-361.
di Pietro, Robert J. 1970a. Review of Muljačić (1969a). Language 46.705-712.
——. 1970b. Review of Lichem (1969). Italica 47.327-329.
Diringer, David. 1953. The alphabet: a key to the history of mankind. New York: Philosophical Library.
——. 1962. Writing. London: Thames and Hudson.
Donzé, Roland. 1967. La Grammaire générale et raisonnée de Port-Royal: contribution à l'histoire des idées grammaticales en France. Berne: Francke. 2nd edition, 1971.
Dostert, Léon. 1972. Descartes on language. In M. E. Smith (ed.):1972:44-49.
Dykema, Karl. 1963. Cultural lag and reviewers of Webster III. AAUP Bulletin 49.364-369.
Eddington, Sir Arthur Stanley. 1958. The philosophy of physical science. Ann Arbor: University of Michigan Press.
Edfeldt, Åke W. 1960. Silent speech and silent reading. Chicago: University of Chicago Press.
Elson, Ben, and Velma B. Pickett. 1962. An introduction to morphology and syntax. Santa Ana de California: Summer Institute of Linguistics.
Esper, Erwin Allen. 1968. Mentalism and objectivism in linguistics. New York: American Elsevier.
——. 1973. Analogy and association in linguistics and psychology. Athens, Georgia: University of Georgia Press.
Evers, A. 1968. Taalkunde en logische relevantie van de dieptestruktuur. Handelingen van het Nederlands Filologen-Congres 30.32-38.
Faust, George P. 1970. Review of Chomsky (1965). General Linguistics 10.43-47.
Foucault, Michel. 1966. Les mots et les choses. Paris: Gallimard.
——. 1967. La Grammaire générale de Port-Royal. Langages 7.7-15.
Foulet, Lucien. 1930. Petite syntaxe de l'ancien français. Paris: Champion.
Francescato, Giuseppe. 1958. Review of Chomsky (1957). AGI 43.66-69.
Francis, W. Nelson. 1958. The structure of American English. New York: Ronald Press.

Fries, Charles Carpenter. 1925. The periphrastic future with *shall* and *will*. PMLA 40.963-1024.
————. 1940. American English grammar. New York: Appleton-Century.
————. 1951. The structure of English. New York: Harcourt, Brace.
————. 1954. Meaning and linguistic analysis. Language 30.57-68.
————. 1961. The Bloomfield 'school'. Trends-Vol. 1.196-224.
———— and Kenneth L. Pike. 1949. Coexistent phonemic systems. Language 25.29-50.
Gans, Eric L. 1981. The origin of language. Berkeley and Los Angeles: University of California Press.
Garvin, Paul L. 1963. Review of R. Jakobson (ed.) (1961). Language 39.669-673.
————. 1970. Moderation in linguistic theory. LSc. 9.1-3.
Gelb, Ignace J. 1952. A study of writing: the foundations of grammatology. Chicago: University of Chicago Press. 2nd edition, 1963.
Gleason, Henry Allan, Jr. 1955. An introduction to descriptive linguistics. New York: Holt, Rinehart and Winston. 2nd edition, 1961.
Godel, Robert. 1957. Les sources manuscrites du *Cours de linguistique générale* de F. de Saussure. Genève: Droz.
Gray, Bennison. 1974. Towards a semi-revolution in grammar. LSc. 29.1-12.
————. 1976. Counter-revolution in the hierarchy. ForL 1.38-50.
————. 1977/78. Now you see it, now you don't: Chomsky's *Reflections*. ForL 2.65-74.
————. 1980. The impregnability of American linguistics: an historical sketch. Lingua 50.5-23.
Greenberg, Joseph (ed.). 1963. Universals of language. Cambridge (Mass.): M.I.T. Press. Second edition, 1966.
Gross, Maurice. 1979. On the failure of generative grammar. Language 55.859-885.
Grunig, Blanche. 1966. La grammaire transformationnelle. La Linguistique 1:2.1-24; 2:1.31-101.
Haas, Mary R. 1941. Tunica. New York: J. J. Augustin. (HAIL 4:1.)
Hall, Edward T. 1963. The silent language. New York: Premier Books.
Hall, Robert A., Jr. 1936. Linguistic theory in the Italian Renaissance. Language 12.96-107.
————. 1938. An analytical grammar of the Hungarian language. Baltimore, Maryland: Linguistic Society of America. (Language Monograph no. 18.)
————. 1942. The Italian Questione della Lingua: an interpretative essay. Chapel Hill, N. C.: University of North Carolina Press.
————. 1944a. Hungarian grammar. Baltimore, Maryland: Linguistic Society of America. (Language Monograph no. 21.)

————. 1944b. Language and super' _ition. French Review
17.377-382.
————. 1948a. Descriptive Italian grammar. Ithaca, N.Y.: Cornell University Press and Linguistic Society of America. Reprinted New York: Greenwood Press, 1974.
————. 1948b. Structural Sketch no. 1: French. Baltimore, Maryland: Linguistic Society of America. (Language Monograph
no. 24.)
————. 1950a. Leave your language alone! Ithaca, N.Y.? Linguistica. (Second edition, under title Linguistics and your
language, New York: Doubleday, 1960 [Anchor Books no. 201].)
————. 1950b. La linguistica americana dal 1925 and 1950. Ricerche Linguistiche 1.273-302. English translation: American
linguistics, 1925-1950, Archivum Linguisticum 3.101-125
(1951)/ 4.1-16 (1952).
————. 1950c. Review of J. P. Soffietti: Phonemic analysis of
the word in Turinese. Symposium 4.441-446.
————. 1951. Review of A. Panzini: Dizionario moderno [and other works]. Language 27.96-99.
————. 1954. Review of Lounsbury (1953). IJAL 20.160-164.
————. 1957. Scopi e metodi della linguistica. AGI 42.57-69,
148-161.
————. 1961. Sound and spelling in English. Philadelphia:
Chilton Books.
————. 1963. Idealism in Romance linguistics. Ithaca, N.Y.:
Cornell University Press.
————. 1964. Introductory linguistics. Philadelphia: Chilton
Books.
————. 1964/65. Review of Piron (ed.) (1961). RPh. 18.511-512.
————. 1965. Fact and fiction in grammatical analysis. FouL
1.337-345.
————. 1966. Pidgin and creole languages. Ithaca, N.Y.: Cornell University Press.
————. 1967. Review of Lepscky (1966). International Review of
Applied Linguistics 5.148-150.
————. 1968a. An essay on language. Philadelphia: Chilton
Books.
————. 1968b. Review of R. M. W. Dixon: What IS language?
FouL 4.87-96.
————. 1968c. L'approccio scientifico nella linguistica de-
sceittiva. Bollettino della Società di Linguistica Italiana
1.45-52.
————. 1969a. Essentials of English phrase- and clause-struc-
ture in diagrams (with commentary). Philadelphia: Chilton
Books.
————. 1969b. Some recent developments in American linguistics.
Neuphilologische Mitteilungen 70.192-227.
————. 1969/70. Review of W. Hirtle: The simple and progressive
forms. RPh. 23.230-234.
————. 1970. Some recent studies on Port-Royal and Vaugelas.
AcLHa. 12.207-233.
————. 1971a. La struttura dell'italiano. Roma: Armando.

————. 1971b. The syllable in Italian phonology. Linguistics 67.26-33.

————. 1972a. The place of rules in linguistic analysis. In M. E. Smith (ed.) 1972:41-43.

————. 1972b. Why a structural semantics is impossible. LSc. 21.1-6. Reprinted in Hall (1978a:85-95).

————. 1972c. Review of Saltarelli (1970). Italica 49.267-272.

————. 1974. Comparative Romance grammar: I. External history of the Romance languages. New York: American Elsevier.

————. 1975a. The nature of linguistic norms. LSc. 34.11-12.

————. 1975b. Review of Vachek (1973). Language 51.461-465. Reprinted in Hall (1978a:128-133).

————. 1975c. Stormy petrel in linguistics. Ithaca, N.Y.: Spoken Language Services.

————. 1975d. Review of Dàrdano (1973). Language 51.211-215.

————. 1976. American linguistics 1925-1969. Darmstadt: Wissenschaftliche Buchgesellschaft.

————. 1977a. Some critiques of Chomskyan theory. NM 78.86-93. Russian translation: Критика теории Хомского. Вопросы Языкознания 1978:5.55-65.

————. 1977b. Italian *pregno*, Eng. *preggy*, and derivational morphology. LSc. 46.24-26.

————. 1978a. Language, literature and life. Lake Bluff, Illinois: Jupiter Press. (ESMS no. 5.)

————. 1978b. Review of L. Fietz: Funktionaler Strukturalismus. Western Humanities Review 32.184-186.

————. 1979. Once more: what *IS* literature? MLJ 63.91-98.

————. 1980. Stormy petrel flies again. Watkins Glen, N.Y.: American Life Foundation.

Halle, Morris. 1962. Phonology in a generative grammar. Word 18.54-72.

Hammarström, Göran. 1971. The problem of nonsense linguistics. ASLU NS.2:4.99-109.

————. 1973. Generative phonology: a critical appraisal. Phonetica 27.157-184.

————. 1976. Linguistic units and items. Berlin: Springer.

Harnois, Guy. 1928. Les théories du langage en France de 1660 à 1821. Paris: Les Belles Lettres.

Harris, James Wesley. 1969. Spanish phonology. Cambridge (Mass.): M.I.T. Press.

Harris, Zellig Sabbetai. 1944. Simultaneous components in phonology. Language 20.181-205.

————. 1951. Methods in structural linguistics. Chicago: University of Chicago Press.

Hathaway, Baxter L. 1967. A transformational syntax: the grammar of modern American English. New York: Ronald Press.

Hawkey, Richard L. 1970. A critique of certain basic theoretical notions in Chomsky's *Syntactic Structures*. FolL 4.198-209.

Hebb, Donald C., Wallace B. Lambert and G. Richard Tucker. 1971. Language, thought and experience. MLJ 55.212-222.

Herdan, Gustav. 1967. The crisis in modern general linguistics. La Linguistique 2:1.27-33.

————. "Götzendämmerung" at M.I.T. Zeitschrift für Phonetik, Sprachwissenschaft und allgemeine Kommunikationsforschung 21.223-231.
Hill, Archibald A. 1961. Grammaticality. Word 17.1-10.
————. 1962a. A postulate for linguistics in the sixties. Language 38.345-351.
———— (ed.). 1962b. Proceedings of the Third Texas Conference on Problems of Linguistic Analysis in English. Austin, Texas: University of Texas Press.
————. 1966. The promises and limitations of the newest type of grammatical analysis. Cincinnati: University of Cincinnati.
Hockett, Charles F. 1948. Implications of Bloomfield's Algonquian studies. Language 24.117-131. Reprinted in Hockett (ed.) 1970:495-514.
————. 1954. Two models of grammatical description. Word 10.210-234.
————. 1955. A manual of phonology. Bloomington, Indiana: Indiana University Publications in Anthopology and Linguistics, Memoir no. 11.
————. 1958. A course in modern linguistics. New York: Macmillan.
————. 1961. Grammar for the hearer. In Jakobson (ed.) 1964: 220-236.
————. 1965. Sound change. Language 41.185-204.
————. 1966. Language, mathematics and linguistics. In Sebeok (ed.) 1966:155-304. Also separately (with new preface), The Hague: Mouton, 1967 (JL-SMi. no. 60).
————. 1968. The state of the art. The Hague: Mouton. (JL-SMi. no. 73.) Italian translation: La linguistica americana contemporanea (Bari, Universale Laterza, 1970).
———— (ed.). 1970. A Leonard Bloomfield anthology. Bloomington, Indiana: Indiana University Press.
————. 1973a. Man's place in nature. New York: McGraw-Hill.
————. 1973b. Yokuts as a testing-ground for linguistic method. IJAL 39.63-79.
————. 1977. Review of T. A. Sebeok (ed.): Current Trends in Linguistics, vol. 12. Current Anthropology 18.78-82.
Hook, Sidney. 1969. The barbarism of virtue. PMLA 84.465-475.
Householder, Fred W., Jr. 1965. On some recent claims in phonological theory. Journal of Linguistics 1.13-34.
————. 1966. [Rejoinder.] Journal of Linguistics 2.99-100.
————. 1972. The principal step in linguistic change. LSc. 20.1-5.
Hymes, Dell H. 1964. Directions in (ethno-)linguistic theory. AA NS.66:3.2.6-56.
———— (ed.). 1974. Studies in the history of linguistics: traditions and paradigms. Bloomington, Indiana: Indiana University Press.
Karrer, Wolfgang, and Edward Palascak. 1976. A Chomsky bibliography. LSc. 40.8-16.
Kates, Carol A. 1976. A critique of Chomsky's theory of grammatical competence. ForL 1.15-24.

Katz, Jerrold J. 1964. Mentalism in linguistics. Language 40.124-137.
————. 1963. The structure of a semantic theory. Language 39.170-210.
Kenyon, John S. 1924. American pronunciation. Ann Arbor: Wahr.
Keyser, Samuel Jay. 1963. Review of H. Kurath and R. I. McDavid Jr.: The pronunciation of English in the Atlantic states. Language 39.303-326.
King, Robert Desmond. 1969. Historical linguistics and generative grammar. Englewood Cliffs, N.J.: Prentice-Hall.
Koutsoudas, Andreas. 1963. The morpheme reconsidered. IJAL 29.160-170.
Kuhn, Thomas S. 1961. The structure of scientific revolutions. Chicago: University of Chicago Press.
Kukenheim, Louis. 1962. Esquisse historique de la linguistique française et de ses rapports avec la linguistique générale. Leiden: Universitaire Pers. Deuxième édition, revue, corrigée et augmentée, 1966.
Lakoff, George. 1969. Empiricism without facts. FouL 5.118-127.
Lakoff, Robin. 1969. Review of Brekle (ed.) (1966). Language 45.343-364.
Lamb, Sydney M. 1967. Review of Chomsky (1964b, 1965). AA NS.69.411-415.
————. 1975. On thrashing classical phonemics. Second LACUS Forum 154-163.
Langacker, Ronald. 1968. Observations on French possessives. Language 54.51-75.
Laghlin, Robert M. 1973. The great Tzotzil dictionary of San Lorenzo Zinacantán. Washington, D.C.: Smithsonian Institution. (Smithson Contributions to Anthropology, no. 19.)
Laycock, Donald C. 1960. Language and society. Lingua 9.16-29.
Lees, Robert B. 1957. Review of Chomsky (1957a). Language 33.375-408.
————. 1960. The grammar of English nominalizations. Bloomington, Indiana: Indiana University Research Center in Anthopology, Folklore and Linguistics, Publication no. 12. (Supplement to IJAL 26:3.)
————. 1963. The promise of transformational grammar. College English 52.327-330, 345.
Leitch, Vincent B. 1982. Deconstructive criticism: theory and practice. New York: Columbia University Press.
LePage, Robert Brock. 1971. Review of L. G. Kelly (ed.): The description and measurement of bilingualism. Lingua 16.427-433.
Lepscky, Giulio C. 1966. La linguistica strutturale. Torino: Einaudi.
Leroy, Maurice. 1963. Les grands courants de la linguistique moderne. Bruxelles: Editions de l'Université de Bruxelles. English translation: Main trends in modern linguistics (Berkeley and Los Angeles: University of California Press).
Levitt, Jesse. 1968. The *Grammaire des grammaires* of Girault-Duvivier: a study of nineteenth-century French. The Hague: Mou-

ton. (JL-SMa. no. 19.)

Lichem, Klaus. 1963. Phonetik und Phonologie des heutigen Ita-
lienisch. München: Hueber.

Lida de Malkiel, María Rosa. 1948/49. 'Saber' y 'soler' en las
lenguas romances y sus antecedentes grecolatinos. RPh.
2.269-283.

Lightner, Theodore. 1975. The rôle of derivational morphology in
generative grammar. Language 51.617-638.

Lobdell, Jared (ed.). 1975. A Tolkien compass. LaSalle, Illinois: Open Court.

—————. 1981. England and always: Tolkien's world of the rings.
Grand Rapids, Michigan: Eerdmans.

Longacre, Robert E. 1964. Grammar discovery procedures. The
Hague: Mouton. (JL-SMi. no. 33.)

—————. 1967. Reply to Postal (1966). IJAL 33.323-328.

Lounsbury, Floyd. 1953. Oneida verb morphology. New Haven: Yale
University Press.

MacCorquodale, Kenneth. 1970. On Chomsky's review of Skinner's
Verbal Behavior. JAEB 13.83-99.

MacMurray, John. 1935. Reason and emotion. London: Faber and
Faber.

Maher, J. Peter. 1973. Review of R. P. Stockwell and R. K. S.
Macaulay: Linguistic change and generative theory. LSc.
25.47-52.

—————. 1974. Review of Bierwisch (1971). HiL 1.399-405.

—————. 1976. The *d* of *sound* and nonstandard *drownd*. LSc.
39.19-20.

Makkai Ádám. 1974. Madison-Avenue advertising: a scenario.
First LACUS Forum 197-208.

Makkai, Valerie Becker. 1974. "Pretty damn seldom ... ": on the
grammaticality of ungrammatical sentences. First LACUS Forum
386-392.

Malkiel, Yakov. 1960/61. Necrology: Leo Spitzer. RPh.
14.362-364.

Malmberg, Bertil. 1942/43. A propos du système phonologique de
l'italien. AcLHa. 3.34-43.

Mandelbaum, D. (ed.). 1949. Selected writings of Edward Sapir.
Berkeley, Calif.: University of California Press.

Martinet, André. 1949. About structural sketches. Word 5.13-35.

Matthews, Peter H. 1967. Review of Chomsky (1965). Journal of
Linguistics 3.119-152.

McCawley, James D. 1969. Lexical insertion in a transformational
grammar without deep structure. PRM-CLS[4] 71-80.

—————. 1975. Madison Avenue, sí; Pennsylvania Avenue, no!.
Second LACUS Forum 17-28.

—————. 1980. Review of Newmeyer (1980). Linguistics 18.911-930.

Meid, Wolfgang. 1966. Review of Hall (1964). Die Sprache
12.100-102.

Meyer-Lübke, Wilhelm. 1936. Romanisches etymologisches Wörter-
buch. 3rd ed. Heidelberg: Winter.

Mok, Q. J. M. 1968. Vaugelas et la "désambigüisation" de la
parole. Lingua 21.303-321.

Morris, Christopher. 1982. Deconstruction: theory and practice. New York and London: Methuen.

Muljačić, Žarko. 1969a. Fonologia generale e fonologia dell'italiano. Bologna: Il Mulino.

————. 1969b. Review of Lichem (1969). Romanistisches Jahrbuch 20.168-172.

Mumford, Lewis. 1961. The city in history: its origins, its transformations and its prospects. New York: Harcourt, Brace and World.

Newman, Stanley S. 1944. Yokuts language of California. New York: Viking Fund.

Newmeyer, Frederick J. 1980. Linguistic theory in America: the first quarter century of transformational generative grammar. New York: Academic Press.

Nida, Eugene A. 1946. Morphology: the descriptive analysis of words. Ann Arbor: University of Michigan Press. 2nd edition, 1949.

————. 1947. Bible translating. New York: American Bible Society.

————. 1951. An outline of descriptive syntax. Glendale, California: Summer Institute of Linguistics.

————. 1964. Toward a science of translating. Leiden: Brill.

Noss, Richard B. 1972. The ungrounded transformer. LSc. 23.8-14.

Nyrop, Kristoffer. 1925. Grammaire historique de la langue française. Vol. 5. Copenhague: Gyldendalske Boghandel.

Ong, Walter J. 1982. Orality and literacy: the technologizing of the word. New York and London: Methuen.

Paden, William D. 1983. Europe from Latin to vernacular in epic, lyric, romance. In Performance of Literature in Historial Perspective 67-105 (Lanham, Maryland: University Press of America).

Panconcelli-Calzia, Guido. 1911. L'italiano. Leipzig und Berlin: Teubner.

Pap, Leo. 1976. Linguistic terminology as a source of verbal fictions. LSc. 37.13-16.

Partridge, Eric. 1970. A dictionary of slang and unconventional English. 7th ed. New York: MacMillan.

Peng, Fred C. C. 1974. The place of generative phonology in the history of linguistics. First LACUS Forum 81-119.

————. 1975. On the fallacy of language innatism. LSc. 37.13-16.

Percival, W. Keith. 1972. On the non-existence of Cartesian linguistics. In R. J. Butler (ed.): Cartesian Studies 137-145 (Oxford [England]: Blackwell).

————. 1976. The notion of usage in Vaugelas and the Port-Royal grammar. In H. Parret (ed.): History of Linguistic Thought and Contemporary Linguistics 374-382 (Berlin and New York: De Gruyter).

Pike, Kenneth Lee. 1943. Phonetics. Ann Arbor: University of Michigan Press.

————. 1947a. Phonemics. Ann Arbor: University of Michigan Press.

————. 1947b. Grammatical prerequisites to phonemic analysis. Word 3.155–172.

————. 1954. Language in relation to a unified theory of the structure of human behavior. Glendale, California: Summer Institute of Linguistics. 2nd edition: The Hague, Mouton, 1967 (JL-SMa. no. 24.)

————. 1964. More on grammatical prerequisites. Word 8.106–121.

————. 1982. Linguistic concepts: an introduction to tagmemics. Lincoln, Nebraska, and London: University of Nebraska Press.

Pilch, Herbert. 1963. Sprachtheoretische Grundlagen der maschinellen Übersetzung. ASNS 200.13–36.

Piron, Maurice (ed.). 1961. A. R. J. Turgot: Etymologie. Brugge: Uitgave "De Tempel".

Pisani, Vittore. 1971. Review of Hall (1971a). Paideia 26.219–223.

Porru, Giulia. 1939. Über die Phonologie des Italienisches [sic!]. Travaux du Cercle Linguistique de Prague 8.187–208.

Postal, Paul. 1964. Underlying and superficial linguistic structure. Harvard Educational Review 34.246–266.

————. 1966. Review of Longacre (1964). IJAL 32.93–98.

Predovich, Ronald. Forthcoming. An aspect of "Cartesian linguistics".

Prideaux, Gary D. 1967. Review of Chomsky (1966a). Canadian Journal of Linguistics 13.50–51.

Pulgram, Ernst. 1967. Sciences, humanities and the place of linguistics. In D. E. Thackrey (ed.): Research: Definitions and Reflections 67–95 (Ann Arbor: University of Michigan Press).

Putnam, Hilary. 1967. The "innateness hypothesis" and explanatory models. Synthese 17.12–22.

Reichling, A. J. B. 1961. Principles and methods of syntax: cryptanalytical formation. Lingua 10.1–17.

Roberts, Paul M. 1963. Corso d'inglese parlato. New York: Harcourt, Brace and Jovanovich.

————. 1966. The Roberts English series. New York: Harcourt, Brace and Jovanovich.

Robertson, Wilmot. 1972. The dispossessed majority. Cape Cañaveral: Howard Allen. 3rd edition, 1976.

Robins, Robert Henry. 1951. Ancient and mediaeval grammatical theory in Europe. London: Bell.

————. 1967. A short history of linguistics. Bloomington, Indiana: Indiana University Press.

Robinson, Ian. 1975. The New Grammarians' Funeral: a critique of Noam Chomsky's linguistics. Cambridge (England): Cambridge University Press.

Rohlfs, Gerhard. 1949–54. Historische Grammatik der italienischen Sprache und ihrer Mundarten. Bern: Francke. 3 vols.

Rommetveit, Ragnar. 1972. Deep structure of sentences versus message structure. Norwegian Journal of Linguistics (NTS) 1.3–22.

Ruwet, Nicolas. 1967. Introduction à la grammaire générative. Paris: Plon.

Sahlin, Gunvor. 1928. César Chesneau du Marsais et son rôle dans l'évolution de la grammaire générale. Paris: Press Universitaires de France.

Saint-Jacques, Bernard. 1967. Some observations about transformational grammar. La Linguistique 2:2.27-40.

Sainte-Beuve, Charles Augustin. 1954 [1840]. Port-Royal. Texte présenté et annoté par Maxime Leroy. Paris: Gallimard.

Saltarelli, Mario Donato. 1970. A phonology of Italian in a generative grammar. The Hague: Mouton. (JL-SP no. 93.)

Sampson, Geoffrey. 1979. Liberty and language. Oxford (England): Oxford University Press.

————. 1980. Schools of linguistics. Stanford, California: Stanford University Press.

Sapir, Edward. 1921. Language: an introduction to the study of speech. New York: Harcourt, Brace.

————. 1925. Sound patterns in language. Language 1.37-51. Reprinted in Mandelbaum (ed.) 1949:33-45.

————. 1929. The status of linguistics as a science. Language 9.207-214. Reprinted in Mandelbaum (ed.) 1949:160-166.

————. 1931. The concept of phonetic law as tested in primitive languages by Leonard Bloomfield. In S. A. Rice (ed.): Methods in Social Science 297-306 (Chicago: University of Chicago Press). Reprinted in Mandelbaum (ed.) 1949:73-82.

————. 1933. La réalité psychologique des phonèmes. Journal de Psychologie Normale et Pathologique 30.247-265. English version: The psychological reality of phonemes. In Mandelbaum (ed.) 1949:46-60.

Saussure, Ferdinand de. 1916. Cours de linguistique générale. Lausanne: Payot. (Later editions: Paris.)

Schane, Sanford A. 1968. French phonology and morphology. Cambridge (Mass.): M.I.T. Press.

Schlauch, Margaret. 1946. Early behaviorist psychology and contemporary linguistics. Word 2.25-56.

Schreiber, Peter A. 1974. Review of Maria Tsiapera: A descriptive analysis of Cypriote Maronite Arabic. Language 50.748-755.

Schwann, Eduard, and Dietrich Behrens (tr. Oscar Bloch). 1932. Grammaire de l'ancien français. Leipzig: Reisland.

Sebeok, Thomas A. (ed.). 1966. Current trends in linguistics. Vol. 3. The Hague: Mouton.

Shippey, Thomas A. 1983. The road to Middle Earth. Boston: Houghton Mifflin.

Skinner, B. F. 1957. Verbal behavior. New York: Appleton-Century-Crofts.

Smith, Henry Lee, Jr. 1968. English morphophonics: implications for the teaching of literacy. Oneonta, N.Y.: New York State English Council.

Smith, M. Estellie (ed.). 1972. Studies in linguistics in honor of George L. Trager. The Hague: Mouton. (JL-SMa. no. 52.)

Snyders, Georges. 1965. La pédagogie en France aux XVIIe et XVIIIe siècles. Paris: Presses Universitaires de France.

Sobelman, Harvey. 1964. Review of R. M. W. Dixon: Linguistic science and logic. Word 20.283-292.

Sommerfelt, Alf. 1938. La langue et la société: caractères so-
    ciaux d'une langue de type archaïque. Oslo: Aschehoug.
Spitzer, Leo. 1943. Why does language change? Modern Language
    Quarterly 4.413-431.
Steiner, George. 1971. Extraterritorial: papers on literature
    and the language revolution. New York: Athenaeum.
————. 1975. After Babel: aspects of language and translation.
    Oxford (England): Oxford University Press.
Stemmer, Nathan. 1973. An empiricist theory of language acquisi-
    tion. The Hague: Mouton. (JL-SMi. no. 173.)
Stockwell, Robert P. 1960. The place of intonation in a genera-
    tive grammar of English. Language 36.360-367.
Strang, Barbara M. H. 1969. Review of Behre (1967). Studia Neo-
    philologica 41.232-234.
Strehlow, Theodore. 1948. Aranda phonetics and grammar. Sydney,
    N.S.W.: Australian National Research Council.
Szépe Gyula. 1967. Review of Chomsky (1966a). Filológiai Köz-
    löny 15.248-251.
Tagliavini, Carlo. 1963. Panorama di storia della linguistica.
    Bologna: Pàtron.
Tekavčić, Pavao. 1972. Grammatica storica dell'italiano. Bolo-
    gna: Il Mulino. 3 vols.
Thass-Thienemann, Theodore. 1973. The interpretation of language.
    New York: Aronson.
Théban, L., and M. Théban. 1971/72. La syntaxe des langues roma-
    nes et l'universalité des structures profondes. Bulletin de
    la Société Roumaine de Linguistique Romane 8.23-36.
Thomas, Lawrence L. 1957. The linguistic theories of N. Ja.
    Marr. Berkeley and Los Angeles: University of California
    Press. (University of California Publications in Linguis-
    tics, no. 11.)
Thorndike, Edward Lee, and Irving Lorge. 1944. The teacher's
    word book of 30,000 words. New York: Teachers College, Colum-
    bia University.
Tolkien, John Ronald Reuel. 1959. Valedictory address to the Un-
    iversity of Oxford [delivered in June 5, 1959]. In Tolkien:
    The Monsters and the Critics 224-240 (London: George Allen and
    Unwin, 1983).
Tovey, Donald Francis. 1956. The forms of music. New York: Me-
    ridian Books.
Trager, George L. 1963. Linguistics is linguistics. Buffalo,
    N.Y.: Studies in Linguistics, Occasional Papers no. 10.
———— and Henry Lee Smith, Jr. 1951. An outline of English
    structure. Norman, Oklahoma: Battenberg Press. Later eds.,
    Buffalo, N.Y. (Studies in Linguistics, Occasional Papers 1.)
Twaddell, W. Freeman. 1972. Syntax, past, present, and future.
    Paper read at the January 1972 Linguistics Meeting of the Eng-
    lish Language Institute, University of Michigan. Preprint.
————. 1973. Straw men and pied pipers. Foreign Language An-
    nals 6.317-329.
Uhlenbeck, E. M. 1963. An appraisal of transformation theory.
    Lingua 12.1-18.

————. 1967. Some further remarks on transformational grammar. Lingua 17.263-316. Lingua 17.263-316.

————. 1975. Critical comments on transformational-generative grammar 1962-1972. The Hague: Smits.

Vachek, Josef. 1973. Written language: general problems and problems of English. The Hague: Mouton. (JL-SC no. 14.)

Vaihinger, Hans. 1924. The philosophy of "as if". London: Kegan Paul, Trench and Trübner; New York: Harcourt, Brace.

Voegelin, Charles F., and Florence M. Voegelin. 1963. On the history of structuralizing in America. Anthropological Linguistics 3:1.12-37.

von Raffler - Engel, Walburga. 1966. L'intonazione come prima espressione linguistica dell'infante. Il Lattante 37:1.29-36.

————. 1970. The L.A.D., our underlying unconscious, and more on "felt sets". LSc. 13.15-18.

————. 1972. The relationship of intonation to first vowel articulation in infants. Proceedings of the International Symposium on Ontology (Acta Universitatis Carolinae [Prague], Philologica I, Phonetica III) 197-202.

————. 1974. Theoretical phonology and first language acquisition. FolL 4.316-329.

Vorster, Jan. 1975. Mommy linguist: the case for motherese. Lingua 37.281-312.

Vossler, Karl. 1904. Positivismus und Idealismus in der Sprachwissenschaft. Heidelberg: Winter.

————. 1905. Sprache als Schöpfung und Entwicklung. Heidelberg: Winter.

Wagner, K. H. 1969. Analogical change reconsidered in the framework of generative phonology. FolL 3.228-241.

Watson, George. 1982. La nouvelle critique: portrait of a dinosaur. L'approche historique en critique littéraire 59-70 (Publications de l'Institut de Littérature, Université Catholique de Louvain, Fascicule 7.).

Weinrich, Harald. 1966. Linguistik der Lüge. Heidelberg: L. Schneider.

Wescott, Roger W. 1980. Sound and sense: linguistic essays on phonosemic subjects. Lake Bluff, Illinois: Jupiter Press. (ESMS no. 8.)

West, Richard C. 1975. The interlace structure of The Lord of the Rings. In Lobdell (ed.) 1975:77-94.

Whitney, William Dwight. 1875. The life and growth of language. New York: Appleton. Reprinted, New York: Dover Books, 1979.

Wiest, William M. 1967. Some recent criticism of behaviorism and learning theory, with special reference to Breger and McGaugh and to Chomsky. Psychological Bulletin 67.214-225.

Winter, Werner. 1965. Transforms without kernels? Language 41.484-489.

Yngve, Victor. 1974. The dilemma of contemporary linguistics. First LACUS Forum 1-16.

Zehnder, Joseph. 1939. Les Origini della lingua italiana de Gilles Ménage. Paris: J. Flory.

Zimmer, Karl. 1968. Review of Chomsky (1966a). IJAL 34.290-303.

INDEX OF NAMES AND TOPICS

In the CURRENT ISSUES IN LINGUISTIC THEORY (CILT) series (Series Editor: E.F. Konrad Koerner) the following volumes have been published thus far, and will be published during 1987:

1. KOERNER, E.F. Konrad (ed.): *THE TRANSFORMATIONAL-GENERATIVE PARADIGM AND MODERN LINGUISTIC THEORY.* Amsterdam, 1975.
2. WEIDERT, Alfons: *Componential Analysis of Lushai Phonology.* Amsterdam, 1975.
3. MAHER, J. Peter: *Papers on Language Theory and History I: Creation and Tradition in Language.* Foreword by Raimo Anttila. Amsterdam, 1977.
4. HOPPER, Paul J. (ed.): *STUDIES IN DESCRIPTIVE AND HISTORICAL LINGUISTICS: Festschrift for Winfred P. Lehmann.* Amsterdam, 1977. Out of print.
5. ITKONEN, Esa: *Grammatical Theory and Metascience: A critical investigation into the methodological and philosophical foundations of 'autonomous' linguistics.* Amsterdam, 1978.
6. SLAGLE, Uhlan V. & Raimo ANTTILA: taken from the program.
7. MEISEL, Jürgen M. & Martin D. PAM (eds.): *LINEAR ORDER AND GENERATIVE THEORY.* Amsterdam, 1979.
8. WILBUR, Terence H.: *Prolegomena to a Grammar of Basque.* Amsterdam, 1979.
9. HOLLIEN, Harry & Patricia (eds.): *CURRENT ISSUES IN THE PHONETIC SCIENCES, Proceedings of the IPS-77 Congress, Miami Beach, Fla., 17-19 December 1977.* Amsterdam, 1979. 2 vols.
10. PRIDEAUX, Gary (ed.): *PERSPECTIVES IN EXPERIMENTAL LINGUISTICS. Papers from the University of Alberta Conference on Experimental Linguistics, Edmonton, 13-14 Oct. 1978.* Amsterdam, 1979.
11. BROGYANYI, Bela (ed.): *STUDIES IN DIACHRONIC, SYNCHRONIC, AND TYPOLOGICAL LINGUISTICS: Festschrift for Oswald Szemerényi on the Occasion of his 65th Birthday.* Amsterdam, 1980.
12. FISIAK, Jacek (ed.): *THEORETICAL ISSUES IN CONTRASTIVE LINGUISTICS.* Amsterdam, 1980.
13. MAHER, J. Peter with coll. of Allan R. Bomhard & E.F. Konrad Koerner (ed.): *PAPERS FROM THE THIRD INTERNATIONAL CONFERENCE ON HISTORICAL LINGUISTICS, Hamburg, August 22-26, 1977.* Amsterdam, 1982.
14. TRAUGOTT, Elizabeth C., Rebecca LaBRUM, Susan SHEPHERD (eds.): *PAPERS FROM THE FOURTH INTERNATIONAL CONFERENCE ON HISTORICAL LINGUISTICS, Stanford, March 26-30, 1980.* Amsterdam, 1980.
15. ANDERSON, John (ed.): *LANGUAGE FORM AND LINGUISTIC VARIATION. Papers dedicated to Angus McIntosh.* Amsterdam, 1982.
16. ARBEITMAN, Yoël & Allan R. BOMHARD (eds.): *BONO HOMINI DONUM: Essays in Historical Linguistics, in Memory of J. Alexander Kerns.* Amsterdam, 1981.
17. LIEB, Hans-Heinrich: *Integrational Linguistics.* 6 volumes. Amsterdam, 1984-1986. Vol. I available; Vol. 2-6 n.y.p.
18. IZZO, Herbert J. (ed.): *ITALIC AND ROMANCE. Linguistic Studies in Honor of Ernst Pulgram.* Amsterdam, 1980.
19. RAMAT, Paolo et al. (ed.): *LINGUISTIC RECONSTRUCTION AND INDO-EUROPEAN SYNTAX. Proceedings of the Coll. of the 'Indogermanische Gesellschaft' Univ. of Pavia, 6-7 Sept. 1979.* Amsterdam, 1980.
20. NORRICK, Neal R.: *Semiotic Principles in Semantic Theory.* Amsterdam, 1981.
21. AHLQVIST, Anders (ed.): *PAPERS FROM THE FIFTH INTERNATIONAL CONFERENCE ON HISTORICAL LINGUISTICS, Galway, April 6-10, 1981.* Amsterdam, 1982.

22. UNTERMANN, Jürgen & Bela BROGYANYI (eds.): *DAS GERMANISCHE UND DIE REKONSTRUKTION DER INDOGERMANISCHE GRUNDSPRACHE.* Akten, Proceedings from the Colloquium of the Indogermanische Gesellschaft, Freiburg, 26-27 February 1981. Amsterdam, 1984.

23. DANIELSEN, Niels: *Papers in Theoretical Linguistics.* Amsterdam, 1987. n.y.p.

24. LEHMANN, Winfred P. & Yakov MALKIEL (eds.): *PERSPECTIVES ON HISTORICAL LINGUISTICS. Papers from a conference held at the meeting of the Language Theory Division, Modern Language Ass., San Francisco, 27-30 December 1979.* Amsterdam, 1982.

25. ANDERSEN, Paul Kent: *Word Order Typology and Comparative Constructions.* Amsterdam, 1983.

26. BALDI, Philip (ed.) *PAPERS FROM THE XIIth LINGUISTIC SYMPOSIUM ON ROMANCE LANGUAGES, University Park, April 1-3, 1982.* Amsterdam, 1984.

27. BOMHARD, Alan: *Toward Proto-Nostratic.* Amsterdam, 1984.

28. BYNON, James: *CURRENT PROGRESS IN AFROASIATIC LINGUISTICS: Papers of the Third International Hamito-Semitic Congress, London, 1978.* Amsterdam, 1984.

29. PAPROTTÉ, Wolf & René DIRVEN (eds.): *THE UBIQUITY OF METAPHOR: Metaphor in Language and Thought.* Amsterdam, 1985.

30. HALL, Robert A., Jr.: *Proto-Romance Morphology.* Amsterdam, 1984.

31. GUILLAUME, Gustave: *Foundations for a Science of Language.* Translated and with an introd. by Walter Hirtle and John Hewson. Amsterdam, 1984.

32. COPELAND, James E. (ed.): *NEW DIRECTIONS IN LINGUISTICS AND SEMIOTICS.* Houston/Amsterdam, 1984. No rights for US/Can. *Customers from USA and Canada: please order from Rice University.*

33. VERSTEEGH, Kees: *Pidginization and Creolization: The Case of Arabic.* Amsterdam, 1984.

34. FISIAK, Jacek (ed.): *PAPERS FROM THE VIth INTERNATIONAL CONFERENCE ON HISTORICAL LINGUISTICS, Poznan, 22-26 August 1983.* Amsterdam, 1985.

35. COLLINGE, N.E.: *The Laws of Indo-European.* Amsterdam, 1985.

36. KING, Larry D. & Catherine A. MALEY (eds.): *SELECTED PAPERS FROM THE XIIIth LINGUISTICS SYMPOSIUM ON ROMANCE LANGUAGES.* Amsterdam, 1985.

37. GRIFFEN, T.D.: *Aspects of Dynamic Phonology.* Amsterdam, 1985.

38. BROGYANYI, Bela & Thomas KRÖMMELBEIN (eds.): *GERMANIC DIALECTS: LINGUISTIC AND PHILOLOGICAL INVESTIGATIONS.* Amsterdam, 1986.

39. GREAVES, William S., Michael J. CUMMINGS & James D. BENSON (eds.): *LINGUISTICS IN A SYSTEMIC PERSPECTIVE.* Amsterdam, 1987. n.y.p.

40. FRIES, Peter Howard and Nancy (eds.): *TOWARD AN UNDERSTANDING OF LANGUAGE: CHARLES C. FRIES IN PERSPECTIVE.* Amsterdam, 1985.

41. EATON, Roger, et al. (eds.): *PAPERS FROM THE 4th INTERNATIONAL CONFERENCE ON ENGLISH HISTORICAL LINGUISTICS.* Amsterdam, 1985.

42. MAKKAI, Adam & Alan K. MELBY (eds.): *LINGUISTICS AND PHILOSOPHY. Essays in honor of Rulon S. Wells.* Amsterdam, 1985.

43. AKAMATSU, Tsutomu: *The Theory of Neutralization and the Archiphoneme in Functional Phonology.* Amsterdam, 1987.

44. JUNGRAITHMAYR, Herrmann & Walter W. MUELLER (eds): *PROCEEDINGS OF THE FOURTH INTERNATIONAL HAMITO-SEMITIC CONGRESS.* Amsterdam, 1987.
45. KOOPMAN, W.F., F.C. VAN DER LEEK, O. FISCHER & R. EATON (eds.): *EXPLANATION AND LINGUISTIC CHANGE.* Amsterdam, 1987.
46. PRIDEAUX, Gary D., and William J. BAKER: *STRATEGIES AND STRUCTURES: The Processing of Relative Clauses.* Amsterdam, 1986.
47. LEHMANN, Winfred P.: *LANGUAGE TYPOLOGY 1985. Papers from the Linguistic Typology Symposium, Moscow, 9-13 Dec. 1985.* Amsterdam, 1986.
48. RAMAT, Anna Giacalone (ed.): *PROCEEDINGS OF THE VII INTERNATIONAL CONFERENCE ON HISTORICAL LINGUISTICS, Pavia 9-13 September 1985.* Amsterdam, 1987.
49. WAUGH, Linda R. & Stephen RUDY (eds.): *NEW VISTAS IN GRAMMAR: Invariance and Variation.* Amsterdam, 1987. n.y.p.
50. RUDZKA-OSTYN, Brygida (eds.): *TOPICS IN COGNITIVE LINGUISTICS.* Amsterdam, 1987. n.y.p.
51. CHATTERJEE, Ranjit: *Aspect and Meaning in Slavic and Indic.* Amsterdam, 1987. n.y.p.
52. FASOLD, Ralph & Deborah SCHIFFRIN (eds.): *LANGUAGE CHANGE AND VARIATION.* Amsterdam, 1987. n.y.p.
53. SANKOFF, David (ed.): *DIVERSITY AND DIACHRONY.* Amsterdam, 1986.
54. WEIDERT, Alfons: *Tibeto-Burman Tonology. A Comparative Analysis.* Amsterdam, 1987.
55. HALL, Robert A. Jr.: *Linguistics and Pseudo-Linguistics.* Amsterdam, 1987.
56. HOCKETT, Charles F.: *Refurbishing our Foundations. Elementary Linguistics from an Advanced Point of View.* Amsterdam, 1987.